ALL ABOUT
CANNING & PRESERVING

ALL ABOUT
CANNING & PRESERVING

IRMA S. ROMBAUER
MARION ROMBAUER BECKER
ETHAN BECKER

PHOTOGRAPHY BY TUCKER & HOSSLER

SCRIBNER
NEW YORK • LONDON • TORONTO • SYDNEY • SINGAPORE

SCRIBNER
1230 Avenue of the Americas
New York, NY 10020

WELDON OWEN INC.
Chief Executive Officer: John Owen
President: Terry Newell
Chief Operating Officer: Larry Partington
Vice President, International Sales: Stuart Laurence
Publisher: Roger Shaw
Creative Director: Gaye Allen
Associate Publisher: Val Cipollone
Senior Editor: Sarah Lemas
Associate Editor: Anna Mantzaris
Consulting Editor: Barbara Ottenhoff
Art Director: Catherine Jacobes
Designer: Sarah Gifford
Photo Editor: Lisa Lee
Production Manager: Chris Hemesath
Shipping and Production Coordinator: Libby Temple
Production: Joan Olson
Food Stylists: Kim Konecny, Erin Quon
Assistant Food Stylist: Meryl Bennan
Step-by-Step Photographer: Mike Falconer
Step-by-Step Food Stylist: Andrea Lucich

Joy of Cooking All About series was designed
and produced by Weldon Owen Inc.,
814 Montgomery Street, San Francisco,
California 94133

Set in Joanna MT and Gill Sans

Separations by Bright Arts Singapore
Printed in Singapore by Tien Wah Press (Pte.) Ltd.

10 9 8 7 6 5 4 3 2 1

Library of Congress Cataloging-in-Publication Data

Rombauer, Irma von Starkloff, 1877-1962.
    Joy of cooking. All about canning & preserving / Irma S. Rombauer,
Marion Rombauer Becker, Ethan Becker ; photography by Tucker & Hossler.
    p. cm. — (Joy of cooking all about series)
    Includes index.
    ISBN 0-7432-1502-8
    1. Canning and preserving. I. Becker, Marion Rombauer.
II. Becker, Ethan. III. Title. IV. Series.
TX603 .R65 2002
641.4′2—dc21
                                              2001058192

Photo shown on half title page: *High-Pectin Fruits,* 44
Recipe shown on title page: *Five Fruits Jam Cockaigne,* 53

CONTENTS

FOREWORD

"...Shelves of glistening, jewel-like jars, filled with canned fruits and vegetables, all labeled, dated and ready to use...." With that simple description in an early edition of Joy of Cooking, *Mom and Granny Rom eloquently summed up the rewards that come from canning and preserving.*

Putting up food for future enjoyment is a decidedly old-fashioned pursuit. Yet, it's one that more and more cooks today are rediscovering. That is why we've devoted an entire volume to the subject in the new All About series. On the pages that follow, you'll find everything you need to know to can and preserve all kinds of foods efficiently, safely, and with delicious results. The outcome is sure to be a rainbow of jars that will brighten your kitchen or pantry shelves.

Most of the recipes in this collection were prepared for the 1997 edition of the Joy of Cooking. *For reasons of space, they were omitted and appear in print here for the first time. Just as our family has done for generations, we have worked to make this version of* JOY *a little bit better than the last. Since 1931, the* Joy of Cooking *has constantly evolved. And now, the All About series has taken* JOY *to a whole new stage, as you will see from the beautiful color photographs of finished recipes and clearly illustrated instructions for preparing and serving them. Granny Rom and Mom would have been delighted.*

I'm sure you'll find All About Canning & Preserving to be both a useful and an enduring companion in your kitchen.

Enjoy!

Ethan Becker pictured with his grandmother, Irma von Starkloff Rombauer (left), and his mother, Marion Rombauer Becker (right). Irma Rombauer published the first Joy of Cooking at her own expense in 1931. Marion Rombauer Becker became coauthor in 1951. JOY as it has progressed through the decades (from top left to bottom right): the 1931 edition with Marion's depiction of St. Martha of Bethany, said to be the patron saint of cooking, "slaying the dragon of kitchen drudgery"; the 1943 edition; the 1951 edition; the 1962 edition; the 1975 edition; and the 1997 edition.

About Canning & Preserving

Canning and preserving foods are ancient pursuits. Once necessities, canning, drying, salting, and pickling practically became lost arts with the advent of refrigeration and the modern supermarket. These days, however, canning and preserving are quickly making a comeback in kitchens across America. The rewards are superb, fresh-tasting foods year round, and the satisfaction of offering such luxuries to family and friends.

Interesting information and tasty recipes are provided under the topics of salting and drying, but because the easiest and most common form of preserving food is the canning method, we make it our primary focus.

CANNING

Every grocery store in America offers aisles and aisles of canned goods from jellies, jams, and preserves to pickles, tomatoes, and beans. So why, you may ask, take the time and energy to can at home?

Fruits and vegetables that you've prepared and canned yourself can be as nutritious and flavorful as most produce found in the supermarket, and the savings can be as high as 50 percent (if you count your time as a labor of love).

Canning is a simple procedure. The following will give you a quick walk through the canning process, and this chapter will then detail each and every step, the equipment and utensils, and safety precautions.

The Canning Process

The term *canning* is somewhat misleading, since most "putting up" of food at home is done in specially designed glass jars, rather than metal cans. Raw or cooked food is packed into these jars with enough liquid to eliminate most of the air space. The jars are then heated—or processed—in one of two types of canners: a boiling-water canner (used for high-acid foods including most fruits) or a steam-pressure canner (essential for low-acid foods including most vegetables). Processing kills the microorganisms and enzymes that occur in all fresh foods and eventually cause them to spoil. It also forces air from the jars. As the processed jars cool, excess air is expelled, forming a vacuum seal. This all-important seal keeps the foods free from bacteria, which might otherwise enter the jars, contaminate the contents, and cause illness.

Canning Cautions

Great care must be exercised in the canning of all foods. Always remember to follow the directions and processing methods and times in the recipes in this book. Be extra cautious when canning nonacid or low-acid foods to prevent the development of *Clostridium botulinum*, a potentially lethal toxin. Because the spores of botulism may resist 212°F—the temperature of boiling water—low-acid foods must be processed in a steam-pressure canner at a temperature of 240°F for the time required in the recipe.

How can botulism be detected in canned foods? That can prove to be difficult since it may be present even if no odor, gas, color change, or softness in food texture is discovered. The first indicators of spoilage to look for are a broken seal or bulging cap. Become familiar with the guidelines in *Checking for Spoilage*, 19. Never test suspicious canned food by tasting it. A good rule of thumb is **when in doubt, throw it out.**

MODERN CANNING

Today, canning is easy and—when you follow the processing guidelines outlined here in accordance with the USDA's latest *Complete Guide to Home Canning*—absolutely safe. Read carefully this entire chapter, 8 to 19, before beginning your home-canning project. If you live in a high altitude area (1,001 feet above sea level or higher), adjust your sterilizing and processing times accordingly for maximum safety. See *High-Altitude Canning*, 15.

The Two Methods of Canning

There are two basic methods for heat-processing canned foods: **boiling water** and **steam pressure.**

BOILING-WATER METHOD

High-acid foods should be processed in a **boiling-water canner.** Fruits, sweet preserves, relishes, pickles, and chutneys are all considered high-acid foods, which means they are less susceptible to spoilage. The few microorganisms that can spoil these high-acid foods are destroyed in temperatures around 212°F (the boiling point of water at sea level).

STEAM-PRESSURE METHOD

Low-acid foods must be processed in a **steam-pressure canner.** Vegetables, tomatoes—which may range from high to low acidity—and nonacid fruits are low in acid and are host to a wealth of microorganisms, such as *Clostridium botulinum*, that spoil food and can cause illness. The temperature of a boiling-water bath is not hot enough to destroy these dangerous microorganisms, but the temperature of pressurized steam inside a sealed kettle (240° to 250°F) is.

HIGH-ACID FOODS (BOILING-WATER METHOD)

Most fruits, fruit juices, jams, preserves, conserves, marmalades, fruit butters, jellies, pickles, chutneys, relishes, vinegar-based sauces, and tomatoes with added acid.

LOW-ACID FOODS (STEAM-PRESSURE METHOD)

Vegetables, tomatoes without added acid, and nonacid fruits (including figs, mangoes, and papayas without added acid).

Canning Equipment

BOILING-WATER CANNER

This is readily available at kitchen and hardware stores, but any large pot will do, as long as it's at least 2½ inches taller than the jars being processed— 1 inch to accommodate the boiling water covering the jars, 1 inch to allow for the splashing water as it boils, and ½ inch for the rack placed under the jars. The pot should fit just one burner, although the base may measure up to 4 inches wider than the burner. (When a large pan is set over two burners, jars in the middle may not receive adequate heat.) For gas burners, the bottom can be corrugated; for electric burners, it must be flat. The pan lid must be either tight fitting or heavy enough to stay in place over briskly boiling water.

STEAM-PRESSURE CANNER

This is a more complicated and expensive item than a boiling-water canner, but is essential for canning low-acid foods safely.

Read the manufacturer's instructions that come with your canner. A steam-pressure kettle comes with a locking cover that allows the steam generated inside to build pressure and reach temperatures of 240° to 250°F (opposite). Fitted into the cover is a vent and either a weighted pressure gauge or a dial pressure gauge; some steam-pressure canners have both gauges.

A weighted gauge regulates the pressure inside the canner by allowing small amounts of steam to escape each time the gauge rocks or whistles during processing. These gauges are reliable and trouble free; their only disadvantage is that they become less accurate at altitudes above 1,000 feet.

A dial gauge, on the other hand, gives you a precise reading of the pressure inside the canner at any altitude. The pressure inside a canner with a dial-gauge canner is controlled manually by regulating the heat of the burner. Dial gauges must be checked annually for accuracy; most county cooperative extension advisers have a testing gauge against which yours can be measured. If your gauge registers more than 1 pound higher at 5, 10, or 15 pounds pressure, order a new one.

Only buy a canner that bears the Underwriter's Laboratory (UL) seal of approval and was made after 1970. Smaller pressure cookers are unsafe for canning. Always thoroughly check and clean the canner before each use according to the manufacturer's instructions, and store it with the cover on upside down in a cool, dry place with crumpled paper towels inside to help absorb moisture and odors.

JARS

The only jars recommended for home canning are mason type jars manufactured in America specifically for canning. Made of tempered glass, these jars are designed to withstand the intense heat of processing (and the extreme cold of freezing). Canning jars may be reused, as long as they are in perfect condition, do not have uneven rims, and are free of cracks, nicks, and scratches.

Jars used for commercially canned foods are supposed to be used only once and are therefore unsuitable for home canning. Antique and decorative canning jars, as tempting as they may be, should be avoided because they may be improperly tempered, brittle, or have flaws that will cause them to break in processing.

Canning jars come in standard sizes ranging from half-pints to quarts. Half-gallon jars are also available but are difficult to handle; we avoid their use for anything but very acidic juices. Canning jars have only two kinds of mouths, wide and tapered. Widemouthed jars are easier to fill and empty.

LIDS AND RINGS

Canning jars are sealed with two piece vacuum caps consisting of a lid and a metal ring. Use lids only once, but rings may be reused until they start to rust or warp. Read the manufacturer's instructions, as there are small differences in design and use. Older-type domed glass lids and other bail-type or spring-lock lids, one-piece metal lids, and old-fashioned porcelain-lined zinc lids are no longer recommended.

UTENSILS

A jar lifter, for removing jars from the canner, and long tongs or a lid wand to pick up lids from very hot water are essential for safe canning. Several other items will prove to be vital: a jar funnel to keep rims clean when filling jars; a long, thin, non-metallic spatula to remove air bubbles from filled jars; a timer; pot holders, and clean towels. For hot packing foods, you will need a broad, heavy-bottomed stainless-steel

saucepan to cook foods evenly and to prevent discoloration.

Also useful for preparing food for canning are a candy thermometer, a paring knife, a chef's knife, a vegetable peeler, a slotted spoon, a cup-size ladle, a large strainer, a set of clearly marked measuring cups and spoons, a cutting board, a blanching basket, a jar or cake rack, a large colander, a small mortar and pestle, a food mill, a 10-pound kitchen scale, and a permanent marker.

Preparing Jars for Canning

WASHING AND STERILIZING JARS

The first step in any canning project is to wash the canning jars, new lids, and metal rings in hot, soapy water or the dishwasher, then rinse them thoroughly. Food that will be processed for less than 10 minutes—all jellies and some juices—must go into sterilized jars.

To sterilize jars, place them upright in the canner, cover them with hot water, and boil fairly vigorously for 10 minutes at altitudes of 1,000 feet or less (at higher elevations, boil 1 additional minute for each 1,000 feet). Leave the jars in the hot water until needed (they can keep for several hours, but bring to a boil again before filling).

Pour simmering water over the lids in a bowl to soften the sealing compound. The lids must be hot when they go on the jars, but do not boil them or you may ruin the seal. Follow the manufacturer's instructions that come with your lids.

PACKING JARS

There are two basic techniques for packing jars: **cold or raw pack** and **hot pack.** With **cold or raw pack,** hot jars are filled with raw or only partially cooked food and covered with boiling liquid. Rarely used, this method often discolors food after a few months, and some foods, especially fruits, may float in the jars.

Hot pack involves simmering food, then filling hot jars with the heated food and adding boiling liquid. Simmering improves the quality of foods to be canned by forcing air from them. More food then fits in the jar, pieces float less, colors and flavors retain their brightness longer, and fewer nutrients are lost to oxidation. The hot-pack method must always be used for unsweetened fruit and is strongly recommended for all foods processed in a boiling-water bath and for most foods processed in a steam-pressure canner, 10.

With both methods, pack the food lightly in the jars. If food is packed too densely, there may not be enough air in the jar to create a successful vacuum seal. Food, instead of air, may be sucked out of the jar, causing the seal to fail. Pack halves and slices in overlapping layers for the best fit. Always pack solids first before adding boiling liquid.

Follow the headspace recommendations given in each recipe. **Headspace** is the pocket of air between the top of the food in the jar and the underside of the rim that allows for food to expand as it heats in processing and that also forms a protective vacuum when the jar has cooled. If food for a hot pack falls below a simmer, bring it back to a boil before filling any remaining jars. If the last jar is only partially filled, refrigerate it and eat the contents within a few days.

Remove air bubbles after filling the jars (except with juices and sweet preserves) by sliding a clean, narrow rubber or plastic spatula between the food and sides of the jar. (Metal utensils can scratch the glass, making it susceptible to breakage.) Slowly turn the jar while moving the spatula up and down, forcing up any bubbles of air. If the food settles below the headspace, more hot liquid must be added and the bubbles forced up again.

Wipe the rims and threads of the jars with a clean, damp cloth to remove any food that could cause the seals to fail. Set on the lids and screw the rings on firmly. Be sure to stop turning when you feel resistance. If the ring is too tight, the air cannot vent, and the food will discolor in storage—or the lid may buckle and the jar break. If the metal ring is too loose, liquid may escape or the vacuum will be weak, and the seal may fail. You will quickly get a feeling for the right tension as you proceed.

Additives

Salt is optional in canning. It adds flavor but has no effect on preservation, except when used in large quantities for pickling. For cold-packed foods, salt can be added directly to the jars before capping. For hot-packed foods, add salt during cooking. Do not can with salt substitutes; the heat of canning may turn them bitter.

Acid is called for in some canning recipes because it acts as a preservative and can enhance the flavor and color of some foods. When using lemon juice to boost acid content, use only commercially bottled or frozen juice. Its acidity is constant, whereas that of fresh juice varies. Citric acid is derived from citrus fruits. It is found in crystal form as "sour salt" in the kosher foods section at the grocery store. Unlike lemon juice, it adds tang without clouding the liquid.

Use a high-grade **vinegar** with a content of at least 5 percent acetic acid (sometimes labeled 50 grain). Cider vinegar and distilled white vinegar are both recommended (see page 90).

Processing Canned Foods

Whether food should be processed in a boiling-water canner or a steam-pressure canner depends on the acidity of the food. See *The Two Methods of Canning*, 10.

BOILING-WATER CANNING

Unless your canner has a jar rack that will securely hold the jars, place a cake rack on the bottom of the kettle to keep the glass jars from touching the canner. Fill the canner half full with hot water and heat to 140°F for raw-packed foods, 180°F for hot-packed. Have a pot of boiling water on hand to top off the kettle once the jars are loaded. With the jars filled and capped, lower them into the canner with a jar lifter (**1**), allowing space for the boiling water to circulate. Add (**2**) or remove boiling water so the level remains 1 inch above the jars. Cover, raise the heat to high, and bring the water to a rolling boil, adjusting the heat if necessary. (When using a pressure canner as a boiling-water canner, rest its cover on top, leaving the vent wide open.) Set a timer for the required processing time from the moment the water boils, noting any adjustment for altitude (opposite). Check the water level periodically, and keep a kettle of boiling water handy in case the water falls below 1 inch above the jars.

STEAM-PRESSURE CANNING

Detailed directions for the use of this appliance are furnished by the manufacturer and should be followed carefully—especially with regards to the checking of the gauge.

Place a jar rack or a cake rack on the bottom of the canner to keep the glass jars from touching the canner. Then add 2 to 3 inches of hot water and, if desired, 2 tablespoons of white vinegar to help prevent staining on the canner and jars. With the jars filled and capped, lower them into the canner with a jar lifter, allowing space for the steam to circulate. Fit on the lid and lock securely, leaving the vent wide open.

Raise the heat to high, and when steam begins to escape, let it vent for 10 minutes to drive air from the canner; failure to do so will affect processing temperatures and result in unsafe food. After venting, close the vent and bring the canner up to pressure (**3**).

With a weighted gauge (**4**), use the appropriate number of weights, consulting the manufacturer's instructions to learn how your weight should behave when full pressure is reached. With a dial gauge, bring the pressure to 2 to 3 pounds below the goal, then turn the heat to medium until the correct pressure is reached. With either gauge, be sure to adjust for higher altitudes, opposite. Start timing the moment the recommended pressure has been reached.

Always monitor the pressure gauge. You can hear the rocking of a weighted gauge, but a dial gauge must be watched. Should the pressure drop too low, you must regain the full recommended pressure and

then start timing again from the beginning. If the pressure goes past the optimum point, reduce the heat a little. Turning the burner up and down, producing big fluctuations of pressure, can draw food out of the jars and ruin the seals. Try to keep the pressure from exceeding 15 pounds. Pressure canners, especially those made of lighter metal, can be very sensitive to heat. For instance, a boiling pot on an adjacent burner could cause a significant increase in the canner's pressure.

When the timer rings, carefully remove the canner from the burner and let the canner cool until the pressure registers zero—depending on the amount of pressure and size of the canner, this may take up to an hour. Then open the vent or remove the weight. Wait a few minutes more (usually between 2 and 10 minutes, according to manufacturer's instructions) before removing the lid. This cool-down period is calculated into processing time, and shortened or sudden cooling may result in spoilage and broken jars. When removing the cover, tip the steamy side away from you, then set the cover down carefully, gauge side up.

PROCESSING TIMES

The length of time required to process food is determined by the density of the food, how it is packed, the volume and shape of the jars, the method of processing, and the altitude at which canning is taking place (see *High-Altitude Canning, below*). When using jars smaller than a pint, follow the recommended time for pint jars. Quarts often require extra time. Follow the processing time given in each recipe.

HIGH-ALTITUDE CANNING

Canning recipes have been formulated for sea level. At higher altitudes, the temperature of both boiling water and steam are lower. This means that the processing time must be increased when boiling-water canning, and the pressure must be increased when steam-pressure canning in order to can foods safely.

Boiling-Water Canning
1,001–3,000 feet, add 5 minutes
3,001–6,000 feet, add 10 minutes
6,001–8,000 feet, add 15 minutes
8,001–10,000 feet, add 20 minutes

Steam-Pressure Canning
Use the timing given for sea level but make the following adjustments in pounds of pressure:

Dial Gauge
0–2,000 feet: 11 pounds
2,001–4,000 feet: 12 pounds
4,001–6,000 feet: 13 pounds
6,001–8,000 feet: 14 pounds
8,001–10,000 feet: 15 pounds

Weighted Gauge
0–1,000 feet: 10 pounds
1,001–10,000 feet: 15 pounds

3

4

After Processing

COOLING THE JARS

After processing (and, if pressure-canning, depressurizing), use a jar lifter to immediately remove the jars from the canner and set them upright on a cloth, a board, newspapers, or a rack. (Leaving hot jars in the canner can induce spoilage.) Stand the jars with at least an inch between them to allow air circulation, but do not put them in front of an open window or in a draft. (Food that has been pressure-canned will continue to boil vigorously in the jars for a short time, but this will stop as it cools.)

Do not tighten the metal rings, as this could damage the sealing compound and ruin the seal. As the jars cool, you should hear a hollow popping sound, indicating that the vacuum has pulled the lid down into place. Let the jars stand at room temperature for 12 to 24 hours before testing the seals.

CHECKING THE SEALS

To check the seals, remove the metal rings and look to see if the lids curve down slightly. Then press the center of the lid. It should not move. If the lid depresses and pops back up, the seal has failed.

Jars that did not seal properly should be refrigerated at once, then either served within a few days, frozen immediately (make sure there is at least 1½ inches headspace in the jar to allow for expansion), or reprocessed within 24 hours of the original processing.

REPROCESSING

To reprocess, first remove the lid and discard it. Check the surface of the jar where the lid sits for any small nicks that may have caused the seal to fail. Prepare a new lid for processing, and a new jar if necessary. Process the same way, for the same amount of time, watching each step closely to try to determine what went wrong. Reprocessed food does diminish somewhat in quality.

Storing Canned Goods

Before storing your jars, remove the metal rings and wipe the jars clean with a damp cloth. This avoids problems later on with corroded or stubborn metal rings and lets you check to see whether any food is caught between the lid and rim. If you see food on the rim, but the seal is secure, simply mark the jar and serve it sooner rather than later. Double-check the seal by making sure you cannot lift off the lids easily with your fingers.

(See *Checking the Seals, opposite.*)

Label each lid with a permanent marker indicating the date of canning, variety of food, and batch number (if there is more than one batch)—which will be useful if a storage problem later develops.

Keep jars of home-canned foods in a clean, cool (between 40° and 70°F), dark, and dry spot. Dampness can corrode the lids and seals. Heat from a radiator, stove, furnace, or the sun will cause spoilage. Do not

store jars at temperatures over 95°. If the storage place is likely to approach freezing temperatures, wrap the jars in newspapers, set them in heavy cartons, and cover with newspapers and blankets.

After a year, chemical changes will begin to diminish the taste, appearance, and nutritional value of canned foods. Date the jars and, for best results, use them within a year.

RULES FOR SAFE CANNING

- Before you start your canning project, read through your recipe twice and then collect the necessary ingredients, equipment, and utensils.

- Follow the recipes in this book to the letter. They adhere to USDA guidelines.

- Be meticulously clean. Make sure everything that touches the food to be canned is spotless. Wash food thoroughly to remove contaminants.

- Measure and cut food (1) according to the recipe. Don't improvise. Can only as the recipe directs, and do not use a mixture of foods or substitutions. Improvisation and safe canning are incompatible.

- Do not can low-acid foods, such as vegetables, bananas, figs, mangoes, or papayas, in their pureed form. Do not thicken liquids with flour or cornstarch before canning. The density of pureed or thickened food makes it difficult for the heat to penetrate the contents of the jar. Puree or thicken canned foods just before serving, if desired.

- Headspace is the pocket of air between the top of the food in the jar and the underside of the rim that allows room for food to expand as it heats in processing, and that forms a protective vacuum when the jar has cooled and sealed. Strictly observe the headspace recommendations in each recipe. Too much headspace may cause an incomplete vacuum; too little may cause food to boil out during processing. Measure headspace on the outside of the jar from the rim down with a ruler (2). No adjustment of headspace is required for high altitudes.

- Prepare only as many jars as will fit in the saucepan or canner in one load (3). Larger canners of both types can accommodate two layers of half-pint jars. Straddle one jar on top of two, staggering them. A jar rack or cake rack set between the layers is helpful.

- Low-acid foods must be processed in a steam-pressure canner.

- Observe the recommended processing times precisely for each recipe. Adjust processing times for high-altitude canning, 15.

- Remember to dress for safety. Wear long sleeves or oven mitts that can absorb an unexpected burst of steam.

Checking for Spoilage

Before serving home-canned food, inspect for spoilage. Make sure that the lids are tight and that each is depressed at the center, indicating a good seal. If any one of the following indications of spoilage is evident, however, **do not taste the food,** but immediately follow the directions given below under *Handling Contaminated Food and Jars.*

Before opening the jar, check to see if: the lid is swollen or no longer curved down; there are streaks of dried food on the outside that originate at the top of the jar; there is mold on the outside of the jar; bubbles are rising in the jar; liquid or food is seeping from the jar; the color of the food is unnatural, or much darker than it ought to be; the liquid is unnaturally cloudy. **Do not open** if you see any of these signs of spoilage.

When opening the jar, you should hear a reassuring "whoosh" as you pry off the lid. Sniff for unnatural or disagreeable (cheesy or sour) odors; look for spurting liquid, gas, or other signs of fermentation; check for mold—any color, even tiny flecks—on the surface of the food and under the lid; examine the food with a fork for sliminess or other unnatural texture. Discard the jar without tasting as directed below if any of these are apparent. Sometimes, the top of canned fruit in the jar darkens because there is too much headspace, and the fruit is sitting above the level of the liquid. This is harmless if there are no other signs of spoilage. Likewise, dark deposits on the underside of the lid are corrosion from acids and salts and are harmless.

Handling Contaminated Food and Jars

Treat any jar with any of the above conditions as though it contained botulism toxins. **Do not taste!**

Handle the jar so no part of it comes in contact with a surface that may later touch food. If the lid of the jar is still sealed, wrap the jar in a heavy bag and place in a garbage container with a tight-fitting cover.

If the jar is unsealed, open, or leaking, you must detoxify the food before disposing of it, to be certain that no child, pet, or unwary wild animal is accidentally poisoned. Cover the jar with a lid and metal ring and carefully lay it on its side in your canner. Wash your hands thoroughly. Without splashing, add water to cover the jar by at least 1 inch. Cover the pot and boil for 30 minutes. **The food has now been detoxified, but it remains inedible.** When cool, wrap the closed jar in a heavy garbage bag, and dispose of it in a garbage can with a tight-fitting lid.

Make a solution of one part chlorine bleach to five parts water, and use it to thoroughly wash anything—including clothing and hands—that may have come in contact with the jar and its contents. Wet surfaces and equipment with the solution and let stand for 5 minutes before rinsing. Discard sponges, cloths, or other materials you used in cleaning up in a garbage bag. Wash hands again.

UNSAFE CANNING METHODS

Over the years, many unsafe canning practices have developed. No matter what your grandmother may tell you, do not do the following: canning without heat processing (the so-called open-kettle method); steam canning without pressurization; processing jars in an oven, a microwave, a slow-cooker, or a dishwasher (it's been done!), or under the sun; using aspirin and so-called canning powders as preservatives in lieu of processing correctly; and mixing foods in one jar without a proven recipe. (It isn't sufficient merely to use the longer processing time required, since safe processing depends on the density of food, and it is impossible to predict how two or more foods will blend in a jar.)

ABOUT
CANNING
FRUITS &
VEGETABLES

*S*ummertime is the best time of year for those who can and preserve. Boxes of berries and baskets of tomatoes—whether from your garden or the local farmers' market—are preserved at their peak, and then enjoyed year round at the table or shared with friends as treasured gifts.

To discover how easy canning is, start with fruit. Because of its high acid level, raw or cooked fruit can be safely processed in a boiling-water bath without much fuss and with no risk of dangerous bacteria—and the results are delicious.

Green beans, corn, and beets are just a few of the vegetables that are most commonly canned. Unlike fruits, vegetables have low acidity and must be steam-pressure processed. This requires a little more time and effort, but the jars of perfect, ready-to-use vegetables that will fill your pantry are a just reward.

A variety of colorful canned fruit and vegetables

Canning Fruit

Fruit can be canned in water, fruit juice, or sugar syrup, with slightly different results.

CHOOSING COOKING LIQUIDS AND SWEETENERS

When fruit is canned in plain water, the texture softens and the color diminishes within months. A little sweetening helps canned fruit retain color, flavor, and shape, but too much sugar can overwhelm a fruit's natural flavors. We recommend adding the least amount of sugar you find palatable. If desired, add sugar substitutes when serving.

A light sugar syrup is very close to the natural sweetness of most fruits and will preserve the quality of the fruit without adding much more than a tablespoon of sugar to each pint jar. Syrup made with white sugar is the most common. The sugar's lack of color and taste brings the natural flavors of the fruit into sharp focus.

Brown sugar has caramelized undertones that complement some fruits. Mild honey or light corn syrup can be used to replace one-third to one-half the sugar in the syrup, but be aware that honey has its own flavor and that corn syrup is supersweet.

Another sweetening possibility is unsweetened (but naturally sweet) apple or white grape juice, which may be used in place of a light sugar syrup. Putting up fruit in its own juice is also permissible as long as the juice is finely strained and is no thicker than the thickest syrup recommended.

Allow about ¾ cup very light to medium syrup or 1 generous cup of heavy syrup per pint of fruit. The thicker the syrup, the more needed.

PREPARING THE FRUIT

Unless specified otherwise, select firm fruit of perfect quality at its peak of ripeness. The pieces should be as similar in size as possible. Wash thoroughly by scrubbing sturdy fruits with a brush under cold running water and shaking berries and other delicate fruits in a colander in several changes of cool water. Rinse fruits after peeling as well.

PREVENTING DISCOLORATION

To prevent light-colored fruits from discoloring after being cut, give the pieces a quick soak (10 to 20 minutes) in an **antibrowning solution** prepared according to one of the following methods: dissolve 1 teaspoon citric acid in 1 gallon water; crush and dissolve six 500 mg tablets vitamin C in 1 gallon water; or purchase a commercial antibrowning product and follow the manufacturer's instructions. Always drain fruits—but do not rinse—before canning with the desired liquid.

BOILING THE FRUIT

Place the prepared fruit, without crowding, in a broad, shallow pan on a burner. In a separate pan, bring the desired liquid to a boil and pour it over the fruit to cover. Turn the heat to high and, when the liquid starts to boil, set the timer according to the recipe. Stir frequently.

SUGAR SYRUP FOR CANNING FRUITS

Percent of Sugar	Intensity of Sweetness	Measure of Sugar to Make 1 Quart
10%	**Very light:** close to the natural sweetness of most fruits	Heaping ⅓ cup
20%	**Light:** satisfying with sweet fruits	Heaping ¾ cup
30%	**Medium:** perfect for most tart-sweet fruits	1¼ cups
40%	**Heavy:** needed only for very tart fruits	Scant 1⅔ cups
50%	**Very heavy:** cloying	2 cups

Prepare the syrup before the fruit, so the syrup will be ready when the fruit is. Place the sugar in a quart measuring pitcher. Add cold water to make 1 quart and stir until the sugar is dissolved.

Canned blueberries, 25, with yogurt and granola

Guide to Canning Fruits

Please read the directions for safe and proper canning, 8 to 19, and *Canning Fruit*, 22 before proceeding. We note superior canning varieties for each fruit as a guide only; other varieties can successfully as well. Hot pack all fruits except grapefruits and mangoes. Use half-pint, 12-ounce, pint, or quart jars. Processing times are the same for all size jars unless otherwise noted and are calculated for sea level. Adjust for higher altitudes, 15.

APPLES

Apples are excellent fruit for canning. Select crisp, juicy apples, a mix of sweet and tart. Superior canning varieties are Arkansas Black, Golden Delicious, Gordon, Granny Smith, Gravenstein, Liberty, McIntosh, Mutsu, Newton Pippin, Northern Spy, Winesap.
Recommended liquid: water or 10 to 30 percent sugar syrup made with up to one-third mild honey, 22. Wash, peel, and core. Slice ¼-inch thick. Place in an antibrowning solution, 22. Drain. Boil gently in the desired liquid (a little cinnamon, allspice, or nutmeg can be added) for 5 minutes, 22. Pack the hot apples in hot jars, and add the hot cooking liquid, leaving ½-inch headspace, 12. Process for 20 minutes, 14.

APPLESAUCE

Superior canning varieties are Baldwin, Greening, Idared, Jonathan, McIntosh, Newton Pippin, Northern Spy, Rhode Island, Russets, Wealthy, Winesap, Yellow Transparent.
Recommended liquid: water. Prepare the apples as above. Place in a pan with just enough water to keep the apples from sticking (about ½ to 1 cup water per quart of sliced apples). Heat quickly and cook, stirring frequently, until tender, 5 to 20 minutes. Mash or puree; sweeten to taste, if desired. A little cinnamon, allspice, or nutmeg can be added. Bring to a rolling boil and ladle hot into hot jars, leaving ½-inch headspace, 12. Process for 15 minutes (20 minutes for quarts), 14.

APRICOTS, NECTARINES, AND PEACHES

These fruits can superbly, although nectarines sometimes not as well as peaches. Cling peaches hold their shape best. Superior canning varieties for apricots are Early Gold, Moongold, Royal, Wenatchee; for nectarines, Garden State, Stanwick; for peaches, Belle of Georgia, Champion, Elberta, Flamecrest, Golden Jubilee, Indian Free, Madison, Red Haven, White Heath.
Recommended liquid: white grape juice or 10 to 30 percent sugar syrup, 22.
Dip peaches in boiling water; slip off the skins. Wash apricots and nectarines—peeling apricots is optional; do not peel nectarines. Cut the fruits in half and remove the pits. If desired, scrape the red from the cavities—it darkens in canning. For easy packing, cut large halves crosswise into 4 chunks. Place the fruit in an antibrowning solution, 22. Drain. Place in a pan without crowding, cover with the desired liquid, and bring to a boil, 22. Ladle the hot fruit into hot jars, packing the halves in layers, cut side down. Add the hot liquid, leaving ½-inch headspace, 12. Process for 20 minutes (25 minutes for quarts), 14.

BERRIES

All canned berries soften but their flavors remain delicious. They are especially good as a light dessert topping for cakes, ice cream, and waffles. Superior canning varieties are blackberries, blueberries, boysenberries, currants, dewberries, elderberries, gooseberries, huckleberries, logan-berries, mulberries, black and red raspberries, serviceberries, strawberries, youngberries.

Recommended liquid: sweetened juice and water, 22.

Working with 1 to 2 quarts of berries at a time, stem, wash, drain, and trim as needed. Cut in half strawberries that are much larger than the rest. In a shallow bowl, mix ½ cup sugar with each quart fruit. Let stand in a cool place for 2 hours, stirring occasionally. Place the berries without crowding in a large, heavy skillet over high heat. Stir gently until the syrup comes to a simmer, or until tight-skinned berries glisten, indicating that most of the sugar has dissolved. Ladle the hot berries into hot jars, and add boiling water as needed, leaving ½-inch headspace, 12. Process for 15 minutes, 14. Process strawberries for just 10 minutes.

CHERRIES

Sweet and tart cherries are both excellent once canned, and are perfect in pie fillings. Superior canning varieties are Bing, Black Tartarian, Golden Sweet, Hedelfingen, Royal Ann, Van, Windsor, Early Richmond, English Morello, Meteor, Montmorency.

Recommended liquid: water or apple juice or white grape juice or 30 percent sugar syrup, 22.

Stem and wash. Place in an anti-browning solution, 22. Cherries retain color and shape best when unpitted. To prevent unpitted cherries from splitting, pierce completely through each cherry with a clean needle. Drain. In a pan without crowding, combine ½ cup desired liquid with each quart of cherries and quickly bring to a boil, 22. Using a slotted spoon, pack the hot cherries into hot jars, and add the hot liquid, leaving ½-inch headspace, 12. Process for 15 minutes (20 minutes for quarts), 14.

CRANBERRIES

Although firmer when frozen, these make a delicious sauce for poultry and meat. Add finely grated orange zest before serving.

Recommended liquid: 40 percent sugar syrup, 22.

Stem and wash. Bring the syrup to a boil, add the berries, and boil for 3 minutes, stirring frequently, 22. Using a slotted spoon, pack the hot cranberries into hot jars, and add the boiling syrup, leaving ½-inch headspace, 12. Process for 15 minutes, 14.

CRANBERRY SAUCE, JELLIED

The classic accompaniment to Thanksgiving turkey, this is also wonderful served chilled for dessert. Slice and top with whipped cream and chopped walnuts.

Recommended liquid: water.

Stem and wash. In a pan without crowding, mix each quart berries with 1 cup water. Cook until soft, then press through a sieve. For each original quart berries, stir in 3 cups sugar. Boil for 3 minutes, stirring. Ladle the hot sauce into hot wide-mouthed jars, leaving ½-inch headspace, 12. Process for 15 minutes, 14.

FIGS

Canned figs have a beautiful appearance and an excellent texture, but their flavor can fade. Select firm fruits without splits. Acid must be added because figs have borderline acidity. Superior canning varieties are Black Mission, Brown Turkey, Celeste, Dwarf Fig, Everbearing, Gillette, Kadota, King, Lattarula, Magnolia, White Kadota.

Recommended liquid: 20 percent sugar syrup, made with up to one-third mild honey, 22.

Do not stem or peel. Wash. Cover with water and boil gently for 2 minutes; drain. Bring the syrup to a boil, add the figs, and boil gently for 5 minutes, 22. Pack the hot figs in hot jars. Add ¼ teaspoon citric acid or 1 tablespoon bottled lemon juice to each pint jar, or twice this amount to each quart jar. Add the hot cooking liquid, leaving ½-inch headspace, 12. Process for 45 minutes (50 minutes for quarts), 14.

GRAPEFRUITS, POMELOS, ORANGES, AND MANDARINS

Raw-pack only. Superior canning varieties are blood oranges, Satsumas, Valencias.

Recommended liquid: 10 to 30 percent sugar syrup, 22.

Wash, peel, then cut off the white pith. Slice into 1-inch-wide segments, discarding the seeds and membrane.

Bring the desired liquid to a boil. Pack the fruit in hot jars. Add the hot liquid, leaving ½-inch headspace, 12. Process for 10 minutes, 14.

GRAPES

Superior canning varieties are Flame, Glenora, Reliance, Seedless Concord, Thompson.

Recommended liquid: 10 to 20 percent sugar syrup, 22.

Select tight-skinned seedless grapes, ideally picked 2 weeks before the peak of ripeness. Wash and stem. Place in an antibrowning solution, 22. Bring to a boil separately the syrup and a pot of water. Drain the grapes, put in a blanching basket or a sieve, and dip in the boiling water for 30 seconds. Pack the hot grapes in hot jars and add the hot syrup, leaving 1-inch headspace, 12. Process for 10 minutes, 14.

LOQUATS

Tasting of apricot, pear, and orange, loquat pieces are good in winter fruit cups and sauces. Superior canning varieties are Big Jim, Champagne, Fletched Red, Gold Nugget.

Recommended liquid: 20 percent sugar syrup, 22.

Wash, remove the stem and blossom ends, halve, and remove the seeds. Boil gently for 3 to 5 minutes, 22.

Pack the hot fruit in hot jars, and add the hot syrup, leaving ½-inch headspace, 12. Process for 15 minutes (20 minutes for quarts), 14.

MANGOES

Raw-pack only. Borderline acidity makes it necessary to add acid. Superior canning varieties are Fairchild, Keitt, Saigon, Villasenor.

Recommended liquid: 20 to 30 percent sugar syrup, 22.

Select firm, yet ripe, green, mangoes. Wash and score the skin lengthwise in quarters to pull off the peel. Cut the flesh from either side of the pit into ¼-inch-thick slices. Do not use overly fibrous fruit. Cover with water, then drain and measure the water. Make 1½ times as much syrup as water needed to cover the fruit and bring to a simmer in a saucepan. Add the fruit, turn off the heat, and let stand until cool. Using a slotted spoon, pack the hot fruit in hot jars. Add ¼ teaspoon citric acid or 1 tablespoon bottled lemon juice to each pint jar, or twice this amount to each quart jar. Gently boil the syrup for 5 minutes before adding it to the jars, leaving ½-inch headspace, 12. Process for 15 minutes (20 minutes for quarts), 14.

Fruit Purees and Baby Food

Puree any fruit except bananas, figs, mangoes, and papayas, which are insufficiently acidic. If necessary, sweeten the fruit puree to taste with sugar or honey. If making a fruit puree for baby food, however, do not use honey as it can cause infant botulism.

Recommended liquid: water.

Stem, wash, pit, peel, and core as needed. Place in an antibrowning solution, 22. Drain. Crush slightly or chop. Mix in a pan with 1 cup hot water for each quart of fruit. Cook slowly until soft, stirring frequently. Press through a sieve or puree using the fine blade of a food mill. Sweeten to taste. If using honey, bring to a boil, stirring. If using sugar, boil until the sugar dissolves. Ladle the hot puree into hot half-pint jars, leaving ¼-inch headspace, 12. Process for 20 minutes, 14.

ORANGES, *see Grapefruits, 27.*

PAPAYAS

The texture and color of canned papayas are excellent, and the flavor is intensified. Papayas have borderline acidity, making it necessary to add acid.
Recommended liquid: 20 to 30 percent sugar syrup, 22.
Wash and peel. Halve, remove the seeds, and cut the fruit into ½-inch cubes. Bring the syrup to a simmer in a large pan. Drop in the papaya cubes without crowding, and simmer for 2 minutes. Using a slotted spoon, pack the hot fruit in hot jars. Add ¼ teaspoon citric acid or 1 tablespoon bottled lemon juice to each pint jar, or twice this amount to each quart jar. Add the hot syrup, leaving ½-inch headspace, 12. Process for 15 minutes (20 minutes for quarts), 14.

PEACHES, *see Apricots, 24*

PEARS

One of the most successfully canned of all foods. Pieces are rich in flavor and not too soft. Superior canning varieties are Bartlett, Clapp's Favorite, Duchess, Kieffer, Moonglow.
Recommended liquid: water or apple juice or white grape juice or 10 to 30 percent sugar syrup, 22.
Wash and peel. Halve or quarter and cut out the cores. Place in an antibrowning solution, 22. Drain.

Boil gently in the desired liquid for 5 minutes, 22. Pack the hot pears in hot jars, making 1 layer with cut sides out, heavy sides down, the next with heavy sides up. Add the hot liquid, leaving ½-inch headspace, 12. Process for 20 minutes (25 minutes for quarts), 14.

PINEAPPLE

Recommended liquid: water or pineapple juice or 10 to 30 percent sugar syrup made with up to one-third mild honey, 22.
Wash, then remove the peel and eyes. Quarter lengthwise and slice out the core. Cut into ½-inch-thick slices or wedges or 1-inch chunks. Simmer in the desired liquid for 10 minutes, 22. Using a slotted spoon, pack the hot fruit in hot jars. Add the hot liquid, leaving ½-inch headspace, 12. Process for 15 minutes (20 minutes for quarts), 14.

PLUMS

Superior canning varieties are Burbank, Early Italian, Fellemberg, Greengage, Italian Prune, Laroda, Mount Royal, Nubiana, Santa Rosa, Satsuma, Seneca, Stanley, Victoria; also wild plums.
Recommended liquid: water or 20 to 30 percent sugar syrup, 22.
Stem and wash. Most plums are best canned whole. Prick on opposite sides with a fork to help prevent bursting. Boil gently for 2 minutes in the desired liquid, 22. Cover the

pan and let stand for 20 to 30 minutes. Ladle the hot plums into hot jars, and add the syrup, leaving ½-inch headspace, 12. Process for 20 minutes (25 minutes for quarts), 14.

RHUBARB, STEWED

Superior canning varieties are Canada and Crimson Red, Valentine.
Recommended liquid: own juice or water.
Select tender bright red stalks. Discard the leaves and green parts. Wash and then cut into 1-inch pieces. In a large pan without crowding, combine each quart of chopped rhubarb with ½ to 1 cup sugar. Let stand in a cool place until the juices flow, about 4 hours, stirring occasionally. Slowly bring to a boil. Using a slotted spoon, pack the hot fruit in hot jars. Add boiling water if needed, leaving ½-inch headspace, 12. Process for 15 minutes, 14.

RHUBARB

Botanically a vegetable, rhubarb has stalks that look like cherry-red celery but are less watery. Their flavor is tartness itself with a fruity aftertaste. Field-grown rhubarb is available principally in April and May; hot-house rhubarb is available in some parts of the country year-round. When choosing rhubarb, pick crisp, firm stalks, ideally no more than an inch wide, and the deepest reds in the bin.

Clockwise from top: pineapple, pear, and pomelo

Canning Fruit Juices

Canning fruit juices is practically as simple and every bit as safe as canning whole fruits. Besides the fact that they are intensely delicious and nutritious, home-canned juices can be sweetened to your taste. Select fully ripe, firm fruit. A juice extractor makes quick work of juicing; if you don't have one, simmer the cut-up fruit according to the recommendations in each recipe and strain it through a jelly bag or four layers of damp cheese-cloth lining a colander, 66. For the clearest juice, refrigerate the strained juice for 24 hours, then pour off the clear juice, leaving the sediment behind, and strain it again through a damp coffee filter.

Pour the strained juice into a heavy-bottomed saucepan over low heat and add sugar to taste, if desired. Stir without simmering until the sugar is dissolved. Raise the heat to high and cook, stirring frequently, until the juice almost boils. Overcooking or boiling fresh juice deteriorates the flavor and nutrients, and we recommend temperatures no higher than 190°F. Pour the hot juice immediately into hot pint or quart jars, observing the headspace noted in the recipe. Juices that will be processed less than 10 minutes must go into sterilized jars. Adjust the lids and process according to the directions for canning high-acid foods in a boiling-water canner, 14. Cooking and processing times for clear fruit juices are brief because liquid transfers heat much faster than whole food.

Guide to Canning Fruit Juices

Please read the directions for safe and proper canning, 8 to 19, and Canning Fruit Juices, above, before proceeding. All juices are hot packed in any size jar with a ¼-inch headspace, except where otherwise noted. Processing times are the same for all jar sizes and are calculated for sea level. Adjust for higher altitudes, 15.

APPLE JUICE

Combine very juicy apples, both sweet and sharp: Bramley's Seedling, Cortland, Empire, Mutsu, Sops of Wine, Stayman, Winesap.

Wash and remove the stem and blossom ends. Use a juice extractor or fruit press, or chop the fruit finely in a food processor. Strain, heat to 190°F, and pour the juice into hot, sterilized jars, leaving ¼-inch headspace, 12. Process for 5 minutes, 14.

APRICOT, NECTARINE, OR PEACH PUREE FOR NECTAR

Excellent quality. Can nectar in pint jars only. Use varieties as indicated for canning fruit, 24.

Wash, pit, and coarsely chop. Use a juice extractor, or, in a pan without crowding, mix 1 cup boiling water with each quart chopped fruit. Cook below a simmer until soft, stirring frequently. Press through a strainer or puree using the fine blade of a food mill. Add 1 to 2 tablespoons bottled lemon juice per quart. Sweeten to taste. Immediately pour the hot nectar into hot jars, leaving ¼-inch headspace, 12. Process for 15 minutes, 14.

BERRY, CHERRY, OR CURRANT JUICE

True flavor and color. Use sweet or tart varieties as indicated for canning fruit, 25. Also see Currants, 53.

Wash, stem, and crush berries; or wash, stem, pit, and chop cherries. Use a juice extractor, or cook below a simmer until soft, crushing and stirring frequently. Add water as needed to prevent sticking. Strain and heat to 190°F. Sweeten to taste. Immediately pour the juice into hot jars, leaving ½-inch headspace, 12. Process for 15 minutes, 14.

CRANBERRY JUICE

Much fresher tasting than commercially canned juice.

Wash, stem, and pick over, discarding softened or discolored berries. Mix equal measures of berries and water in a pan without crowding. Quickly bring to a boil, then reduce the heat and cook below a simmer until all the berries have popped. Strain and heat to 190°F. Sweeten to taste. Immediately pour the juice into hot jars, leaving ¼-inch headspace, 12. Process for 15 minutes, 14.

GRAPE JUICE

Superior canning varieties for purple are Beta, Catawba, Concord, Fredonia, Scuppernong; for white, Delaware, Himrod, Seneca, Tokay.

Remove large stems. Wash. Use a juice extractor, or cover in a pan with boiling water and cook below a simmer until soft, crushing frequently. Avoid crushing the seeds (they are bitter). Refrigerate the strained juice overnight and then pour off the clear juice from the sediment. (This is essential for grape juice; otherwise, crystals will form in the juice.) Strain and heat to 190°F. Sweeten to

taste. Immediately pour the juice into sterilized jars, leaving ¼-inch headspace, 12. Process for 5 minutes, 14.

GRAPEFRUIT OR GRAPEFRUIT-ORANGE JUICE

For a grapefruit-orange blend, use equal amounts of each juice. Use varieties as indicated for canning fruit, 27.

Wash. Extract the juice. Strain and sweeten to taste, then, in a double boiler, hold for 5 minutes at 190°F. Immediately pour the juice into hot jars, leaving ¼ inch headspace, 12. Process for 15 minutes, 14.

PLUM JUICE

Superior canning varieties are Au Producer, Elephant Heart, Pipestone, Red Heart, Satsuma, Waneta.

Wash, pit, and chop. Use a juice extractor, or, in a pan without crowding, mix 1 quart water with each quart chopped fruit. Cook below a simmer until soft, stirring frequently. Strain and heat to 190°F. Sweeten to taste. Pour the juice into hot jars, leaving ¼-inch headspace, 12. Process for 15 minutes, 14.

RHUBARB JUICE

Makes a tangy summer cooler. Use varieties as indicated for canning fruit, 28.

Select tender bright red stalks. Discard the leaves and green parts. Do not peel. Chop. Combine each quart chopped rhubarb with ½ cup sugar and let stand in a cool place, stirring occasionally, until the juices flow, about 4 hours. Use a juice extractor, or, in a pan, mix 1 quart water with each 5 quarts fruit. Heat quickly until the water just begins to boil. Strain and heat to 190°F. Immediately pour the juice into hot jars, leaving ¼-inch headspace, 12. Process for 15 minutes, 14.

Canning Tomatoes

Tomatoes are the all-time favorite fruit for home canning. They're abundant in their season, extremely versatile to use, and easy to can.

Tomatoes can be processed by either the boiling-water or steam-pressure method. While the boiling-water method gives good results, we recommend steam-pressure canning for better flavor and nutritional value. Select perfect, firm, ripe—not over-ripe—fruit without soft spots, bruises, mold, or broken skin. Do not can tomatoes from dead or frost-killed vines. Wash the fruit until the rinsing water is clear. Peel tomatoes according to the techniques below. Green tomatoes can safely be canned following any recommendation for ripe tomatoes. However, cherry and grape tomatoes do not can successfully.

Tomatoes have unpredictable acid levels; this is true even of old-fashioned varieties with a high-acid reputation. To be on the safe side, we recommend adding acid to ripe tomatoes, though it isn't necessary for tomatillos or green tomatoes. We prefer citric acid for its lack of flavor, but bottled lemon juice or, in a pinch, 4 tablespoons of 5 percent–acidity cider vinegar per quart jar can also be used (though the flavor of the latter is an acquired taste). A little sugar can be blended into the tomatoes to balance tartness, if necessary, but do not add vegetables or other ingredients that would lower the level of acid. A single small fresh herb leaf, like sweet basil, is acceptable; its flavor will intensify with time.

Tomatillos are small, tart, husk-covered green orbs used widely in Mexican cooking. Though only very distantly related to tomatoes, they are canned by the same methods and with equal ease and success.

HOW TO PEEL TOMATOES

1 Using a small, sharp knife, cut a small X in the bottom of the tomatoes—do not cut the flesh. Ease the tomatoes one by one into a pot of boiling water. Leave ripe tomatoes in for about 15 seconds, barely ripe tomatoes in for twice as long. Lift them out with a slotted spoon and drop into a bowl of ice water to stop the cooking. Alternatively, if the recipe can use a touch of smoky flavor, hold the tomato on a long-handled fork over a gas burner, turning it until the skin splits. Do not plunge in water, but peel the tomato as directed below.

2 Pull off the skin with the tip of the knife. If the skin sticks, return the tomato to the boiling water for another 10 seconds.

TOMATILLOS

Tomatillos look like small shiny green, yellow-green, or lavender tomatoes encased in parchment-paper husks. Tomatillos are picked underripe. They are related to gooseberries and have a lemony tang. This tang lends sprightliness to sauces in Mexican cooking. Tomatillos may be sporadically available at the supermarket, but they are always for sale at Latino groceries. Select fruits that are firm and fill their husks, and avoid any that have come out of them. They can be stored unwashed and unhusked, loose in the refrigerator crisper—they will keep for weeks. Husk but do not peel before canning. Canned tomatillos can be served as a condiment with grilled meats and poultry, and are especially good with grilled fish and shellfish. The flavor of the tomatillo goes well with chili peppers, cilantro, and lime.

Guide to Canning Tomatoes

Please read the directions for safe and proper canning, 8 to 19, and *Canning Tomatoes*, 33, before proceeding. Hot pack all forms of tomatoes in pint or quart jars. After packing in the jar, add ¼ teaspoon citric acid or 1 tablespoon bottled lemon juice to each pint jar, twice this amount to each quart jar. Processing times are calculated for sea level. Adjust for higher altitudes, 15.

TOMATOES, CRUSHED

Superior canning varieties are Bellstar, Campbell 1327.

Wash, peel, cut out the cores, and quarter. Place 1 layer deep in a large pan. Set over high heat and crush with a potato masher or pestle, then stir until boiling. If desired, sprinkle with salt as you go. Gradually add the remaining pieces, stirring constantly—no need to crush. When up to 6 layers have been added, boil gently for 5 minutes, stirring frequently, 22. Pack the hot tomatoes in hot jars, leaving ½-inch headspace, 12. Add the acid to each jar, above. Process pints for 35 minutes in a boiling-water canner, quarts for 45 minutes; or process both for 15 minutes in a steam-pressure canner, 14.

TOMATOES, PACKED IN WATER

Superior canning varieties are Glamour, Heinz 1350 VF, Marglobe, Ole, Pearson, Red Pear, Red Plum, Tappy's Finest.

Wash, peel, and cut out the cores. To can whole tomatoes, select small meaty ones of uniform size. To can halves, cut the tomatoes on a plate to retain juice. Put in a pan without crowding, add water to cover, and boil gently for 5 minutes, 22. Pack the hot tomatoes in hot jars. Add the acid, above, and salt to taste. Add the hot cooking liquid, leaving ½-inch headspace, 12. Process pints for 40 minutes in a boiling-water canner, quarts for 45 minutes; or process both for 10 minutes in a steam-pressure canner, 14.

TOMATO JUICE OR SOUP

Superior canning varieties are Bellstar, Ropreco, Rutgers VF, San Marzano, Super VF Roma. (Photo, 32.)

Wash and stem. Quarter about 1 pound on a plate, retaining the juice. Place in a pan over high heat and crush the tomatoes with a potato masher or pestle as they come to a boil. Boil constantly and vigorously while slowly adding and crushing more fresh tomatoes. If desired, sprinkle with salt as you go. When all the tomatoes have been added, simmer for 5 minutes, stirring frequently, 22. Press hot through a sieve or food mill back into the pan. Quickly boil the juice and immediately fill hot jars, leaving ½-inch headspace, 12. Add the acid to each jar, above. Process pints for 35 minutes in a boiling-water canner, quarts for 40 minutes; or process both for 15 minutes in a steam-pressure canner, 14.

TOMATO-VEGETABLE JUICE OR SOUP

Use tomato varieties as indicated for juice or soup, above.

Weigh the tomatoes. Wash, stem, quarter, crush, and boil as for juice, above. For every 5½ pounds tomatoes, blend in up to, but no more than, ¾ cup mixed finely chopped carrots, celery, onions, and bell or chili peppers. Simmer for 20 minutes, stirring frequently. Press hot through a sieve or food mill back into the pan. Rapidly bring the juice to a boil and immediately fill hot jars, leaving ½-inch headspace, 12. Add the acid to each jar, above. Process pints for 35 minutes in a boiling-water canner, quarts for 40 minutes; or process both for 15 minutes in a steam-pressure canner, 14.

TOMATO PUREE

Use tomato varieties as indicated for juice or soup, above.

Wash, prepare, cook, and strain the tomatoes as for juice, above. Simmer in a large skillet, stirring frequently, until reduced to the desired consistency. Fill hot jars with the hot sauce, leaving ½-inch headspace, 12. Add the acid, above. Process pints for 35 minutes in a boiling-water canner, quarts for 40 minutes; or process both for 15 minutes in a steam-pressure canner, 14.

TOMATILLOS

Tomatillos have a consistently high acid-level and do not need any added acid.

Select firm underripe fruit. Peel off and discard the husks, then rinse off the sticky covering. Run a clean needle through the fruit to prevent bursting. Can as for whole tomatoes in water, above. Leave ½-inch headspace, 12. Process pints for 40 minutes in a boiling-water canner, quarts for 45 minutes; or process both for 10 minutes in a steam-pressure canner, 14.

Clockwise from top: canned whole tomatoes (above), tomatillos, tomatoes

Canning Vegetables

The most important thing to keep in mind when canning vegetables is that they are low in acid—making them highly susceptible to contamination—and therefore must be steam-pressure processed.

PREPARING THE VEGETABLES

Select firm-ripe vegetables of perfect quality, as evenly sized as possible. Discard any with soft spots, bruises, mold, or broken skin. Scrub sturdy vegetables, such as carrots, potatoes, and squashes, under cold running water until clean. Shake and stir small but firm vegetables, such as shelled peas, in a colander under cold running water. Rinse delicate vegetables, such as greens, in several changes of tepid water until the water is free of sand and other contaminants. Rinse vegetables after peeling or shelling as well.

BOILING THE VEGETABLES

Most vegetables for canning are improved by briefly precooking. Place the prepared vegetables, without crowding, in a broad, shallow pan on a burner. Pour enough boiling salted water over them to cover, turn the heat to high, and start timing when the liquid starts to boil. Some vegetables are topped off in the jar with the cooking liquid, while others benefit from the addition of fresh boiling water. Certain vegetables are more apt to be loaded with potential contaminants, which are best tossed out with the cooking liquid.

SELECTING VEGETABLES

The following vegetables are better pickled, frozen, or eaten fresh and should not be used for canning: broccoli, Brussels sprouts, cabbage, cauliflower, cucumbers, eggplant, endive, chicory, lettuce and other salad greens, and root vegetables not mentioned in this chapter.

Guide to Canning Vegetables

Please read the directions for safe and proper canning, 8 to 19, and *Canning Vegetables, above,* before proceeding. Hot pack all vegetables with 1-inch headspace, 12, in half-pint, 12-ounce, pint, or quart jars except where otherwise noted. Processing times are calculated for sea level. Adjust for higher altitudes, 15. We note superior canning varieties for vegetables as a guide only; other varieties can successfully as well.

ARTICHOKES, SMALL GLOBE

Select young, tender buds. Wash. Remove the leaves down to the edible center leaves and then cut off the dark green tops. The trimmed artichokes can be up to 2 inches wide. Boil gently in vinegar water (3 tablespoons cider vinegar per 1 quart water) for 5 minutes, above. Pack the hot artichokes in hot jars. Add fresh boiling vinegar water brined with a rounded 2½ teaspoons salt per quart, leaving 1-inch headspace, 12. Process for 25 minutes in a steam-pressure canner, 14.

ASPARAGUS

Select thick, tight-tipped spears. Wash. For whole stalks, cut 1 inch shorter than the jars. For pieces, remove the tough skin and ends, and cut into 2-inch lengths. Boil gently for 2 to 3 minutes, above. Loosely pack the hot asparagus in hot jars, whole stalks tips up and add the boiling cooking liquid, leaving 1-inch headspace, 12. Process for 30 minutes (40 minutes for quarts) in a steam-pressure canner, 14.

BEANS, SNAP/GREEN

Superior canning varieties for bush beans are Blue Lake 274, Gold Mine, Tendercrop, Topcrop; for pole beans, Blue Lake FM-1, Kentucky Wonder. Select crisp, tender, meaty pods. Wash. Remove the tips and any strings. Leave whole, or snap or cut into uniform pieces. Boil gently for 5 minutes, above. Loosely pack the hot beans in hot jars, standing whole beans on end. Add the boiling cooking liquid, leaving 1-inch headspace, 12. Process for 20 minutes (25 minutes for quarts) in a steam-pressure canner, 14.

Clockwise from left: canned green beans, asparagus, and artichokes

BEANS AND PEAS, FRESH

See also Peas, Green opposite.

A superior canning variety for black-eyed peas is Queen Anne; for butter beans, Dixie; for crowder peas, Calico; for fava beans, Broad Windsor; for field peas, Banquet; for lima beans, Fordhook 242; for soy beans, Butterbean.

Select plump, tender pods. Shell and wash thoroughly. Sort sizes, if necessary. Boil gently for 3 minutes, 37. Loosely pack the hot beans in hot jars, and add the boiling cooking liquid, leaving 1-inch headspace, 12. (Note: Leave 1½-inches headspace for black-eyed, crowder, and field peas in quarts.) Process for 40 minutes (50 minutes for quarts) in a steam-pressure canner, 14.

BEETS

Superior canning varieties are Big Red, Detroit Dark Red, Detroit Supreme, Formanova, Little Ball, Pacemaker III, Red Ace, Ruby Queen.

Select crisp beets up to 3 inches wide. Wash and trim, leaving 1 inch of roots and stems. Boil gently just until the skins slip off, 15 to 20 minutes, 37. Trim the roots and stems flush with the beets and remove the skins. Leave baby, 1- to 2-inch beets whole. Cut tender young beets into 1-inch chunks, larger older beets into ½-inch cubes or slices. Pack the hot beets in hot jars, adding ¼ teaspoon salt per pint. Add fresh boiling water, leaving 1-inch headspace, 12. Process for 30 minutes (35 minutes for quarts) in a steam-pressure canner, 14.

CARROTS

Superior canning varieties are Danvers Half Long, Falcon II, Minicor, Little Finger. Packaged "minis" or "babies" do not can well.

Select sweet, crisp young carrots up to 1¼ inches wide. Wash, peel, and wash again. Carrots up to ½ inch wide can be canned whole; cut to the length of the jar. Cut the rest into ½-inch-wide sticks, slices, or chunks. Boil gently for 5 minutes, 37. Pack the hot carrots in hot jars, and add the boiling cooking liquid, leaving 1-inch headspace, 12. Process for 25 minutes (30 minutes for quarts) in a steam-pressure canner, 14.

CORN, WHOLE KERNEL

Home-canned corn is crisp and sweet. Supersweet or underripe kernels may turn brown, but this is not harmful. Superior canning varieties are Country Gentleman, Flavor Queen, Golden Jubilee, Merlin, Milk 'n Honey II.

Remove the husks and silks. Wash the corn. Drop into boiling water and boil for 3 minutes, 37. Cut the kernels from the cob at about three-quarters the depth of the kernel. Do not scrape the cob—cob material clouds the jars. In a pan, mix 1 cup boiling water (salted to taste) with every 1 quart kernels. Simmer for 5 minutes. Pack the hot kernels in hot jars, and add the boiling cooking liquid, leaving 1-inch headspace, 12. Process for 55 minutes (1 hour 25 minutes for quarts) in a steam-pressure canner, 14.

CORN, CREAM STYLE

Only use pint jars or smaller because the mixture is so dense. Use the same varieties as indicated for whole kernels, above.

Select, husk, remove the silks, and wash the corn. Drop into boiling water as for whole-kernel corn, above. Boil for 4 minutes, 37. Cut the kernels from the cob half the depth of the kernel. Scrape off the remaining kernels and juice with a table knife, but do not include the cob material. In a pan, mix one-half as much boiling salted water as corn and scrapings. Bring to a boil, stirring. Ladle the hot mixture into hot jars, leaving 1-inch headspace, 12. Process half-pints (only) for 1 hour 25 minutes in a steam-pressure canner, 14.

GREENS

The flavor of canned greens is true but the texture soft, making them perfect for soups. A mix gives best results. A superior canning variety for chard is Fordhook Giant; for collards, Top Bunch; for kale, Green Curled; for mustard, Savanna; for spinach, Melody.

Select freshly harvested crisp, very thick leaves. Wash. Cut off any roots, tough ribs, and stems. Leave tender ribs and stems. Drop about 2 quarts at a time into a blanching basket in boiling water—handle with long tongs—and boil until well wilted, 3 to 5 minutes. Loosely drop the drained leaves into hot jars, adding ¼ teaspoon each citric acid and salt per quart. Add fresh boiling water, leaving 1-inch headspace, 12. Process for 1 hour 10 minutes (1½ hours for quarts) in a steam-pressure canner, 14.

MUSHROOMS

This method produces delicious canned mushrooms. **Caution: Do not can wild mushrooms!**

Select unblemished 1- to 1½-inch commercial mushrooms heavy for their size, with tightly closed caps. Trim the stems flush with the caps. Soak caps in cold water for 10 minutes. Wash in fresh water. Cover with cold water and boil gently for 5 minutes, 37. Pack the hot mushrooms in hot jars, adding 1 crushed 500 mg vitamin C tablet (ascorbic acid) and ¼ teaspoon salt per pint. Add fresh boiling water, leaving 1-inch headspace, 12. Process half-pints and pints (only) for 45 minutes in a steam-pressure canner, 14.

OKRA

Canned whole pods are soft but not slimy, and the flavor is excellent. Add to soups and stews just before serving. Superior canning varieties are Annie Oakley II, Red Velvet.

Select young, tender pods. Wash and leave whole. Boil gently for 2 minutes, 37. Pack the hot pods upright in hot jars. Add the hot cooking liquid, leaving 1-inch headspace, 12. Process for 25 minutes (40 minutes for quarts) in a steam-pressure canner, 14.

ONIONS, BOILING/PEARL

The texture of canned onions is soft, but the flavor is good. Lightly brown in oil before serving. Superior canning varieties are Barletta, Crystal Wax, Early Aviv.

Select sweet onions of uniform size, up to 1 inch wide. Wash and peel, cutting a shallow X in the base. Boil gently for 5 minutes, 37. Pack the hot onions in hot jars, and add the boiling cooking liquid, leaving 1-inch headspace, 12. Process for 40 minutes in a steam-pressure canner, 14.

PEAS, GREEN

Superior canning varieties are Alaska Early, Alderman, Victory Freezer.

Using medium to large sweet peas, prepare as for fresh beans and peas, opposite, but bring to a rolling boil and boil for 2 minutes, 37. Pack as for fresh beans and peas, leaving 1-inch headspace, 12. Process for 40 minutes in a steam-pressure canner, 14.

PEPPERS

Only can peppers with extra-thick walls—the rest are too soft. Superior canning varieties for bell peppers are Cherry Sweet, Gambo, Super Red Pimento; for chili peppers, Anaheim TMR, Jalapeño M, Large Red Cherry.

Select crisp, meaty peppers of any color. Wash, roast (below, right), and peel the peppers. Remove the cores and seeds. Leave small peppers whole, slashing twice lengthwise with a knife. Quarter large peppers. Fit the peppers in hot jars, adding ¼ teaspoon salt per pint. Add boiling water, leaving 1-inch headspace, 12. Process half-pints and pints (only) for 35 minutes in a steam-pressure canner, 14.

POTATOES

Canned potatoes are firm and sweet. Superior canning varieties are All Blue, Dark-Red Norland, Kennebec, Rose Finn, Ruby Crescent, Yellow Finn, Yukon Gold.

Select firm, new, waxy potatoes. Leave whole if 1 inch wide, or cut 2-inch potatoes in half. Wash, peel, and wash again. Gently boil ½-inch pieces for 2 minutes, 37; boil larger pieces and whole potatoes for 10 minutes. Pack the hot potatoes in hot jars. Add salt to taste and fresh boiling water, leaving 1-inch headspace, 12. Process for 35 minutes (40 minutes for quarts) in a steam-pressure canner, 14. Note: Potatoes stored below 45°F may discolor in jars, but this is harmless.

POTATOES, SWEET

A superior canning variety is Nancy Hall.

Select tubers up to 2 inches wide, with waxy flesh. Left whole, 3 to 4 fit in a quart jar. Prepare 20 percent sugar syrup, 22. Wash the tubers. Boil gently, 37, or steam until the skins loosen, about 15 minutes. Peel. Fit the hot sweet potatoes in hot quart jars, adding ½ teaspoon salt. Add the boiling syrup, leaving 1-inch headspace, 12. Process for 1½ hours in a steam-pressure canner, 14.

SQUASH, SUMMER

Superior canning varieties are Butterstick, Black Beauty zucchini.

Select very firm young squashes. Wash. Cut into ½-inch-thick slices. Boil gently for 2 to 3 minutes, 37. Pack the hot squash in hot jars, and add the boiling cooking liquid, leaving 1-inch headspace, 12. Process for 30 minutes (40 minutes for quarts) in a steam-pressure canner, 14.

SQUASH, WINTER AND PUMPKIN

Serve mashed with butter and nutmeg. Superior canning varieties are Buttercup, Golden Hubbard; Green Striped Cushaw, Small Sugar, and Sugar Pie pumpkins; Waltham Butternut.

Select small squashes and pumpkins with hard rinds and sweet, dry, thick, fine-grained (not stringy) flesh. Wash and peel. Cut crosswise into 1-inch slices. Remove the seeds and fibers, then cut into 1-inch cubes. Boil gently for 2 minutes, 37. Do not mash or puree. Pack the hot squash in hot jars, and add boiling cooking liquid, leaving 1-inch headspace, 12. Process for 55 minutes (1½ hours for quarts) in a steam-pressure canner, 14.

SUCCOTASH

This traditional American dish (opposite) cans well. The tomato is optional.

Select freshly shelled lima beans and freshly cut whole corn kernels (and tomatoes as directed for crushing, 34). Prepare as directed for each vegetable. In a pan, combine 4 parts lima beans, 3 parts corn, and 2 parts crushed tomatoes. Boil gently for 5 minutes, 37. Pack the hot mixture in hot jars, and add boiling cooking liquid, leaving 1-inch headspace, 12. Process for 1 hour (1 hour 25 minutes for quarts) in a steam-pressure canner, 14.

TURNIPS

Sweet, crisp young turnips remain tasty and firm when canned. Superior canning varieties are Market Express, Purple Top White Globe, Tokyo Cross.

Select tender young turnips no more than 3 inches wide. Wash thoroughly and peel. Can 1-inch-wide young turnips whole. Cut larger turnips into 1-inch cubes. Boil gently for 5 minutes, 37. Pack the hot turnips in hot jars, and add the boiling cooking liquid, leaving 1-inch headspace, 12. Process for 30 minutes (35 minutes for quarts) in a steam-pressure canner, 14.

HOW TO STOVE-ROAST PEPPERS

This is the simplest method for roasting fresh peppers. Place whole peppers directly in the flames of your gas burner on its highest setting. (If you do not have a gas burner, set the peppers on a hot outdoor grill or underneath a preheated broiler.) Keep an eye on the peppers and turn them frequently with tongs, letting the peppers blister (do not pierce, as juices will be lost). Continue until the entire surface is blistered. Lay peppers in a bowl and cover with a plate. Leave for a few minutes, then scrape off the skins with a knife.

ABOUT
JAMS, JELLIES & PRESERVES

*A*n afternoon spent putting up jams, jellies, fruit butters, or other sweet preserves is a satisfying way to expand your pantry, and to savor the taste of seasonal fruit year round. Homemade preserves also make precious gifts, which cannot be duplicated commercially.

Jams, jellies, preserves, conserves, marmalades, fruit butter, and jellied fruit sauces are all based on the principle of cooking fruit with a sweetener—sugar, honey, or fruit juice. The differences that distinguish one from another are in the techniques and ingredients used. Jelly has great clarity as it is made from strained juice cooked with sugar until firm. Preserves, marmalades, and conserves are bits of fruit cooked to a translucent state in a sugar syrup. Jams, fruit butters, and jellied fruit sauces are purees of progressively increasing density.

From left: *Plum Jam, 54; Bitter Orange Marmalade, 79; Cranberry Conserves, 63*

Selecting Fruit

Choose only the freshest and most flavorful fruit for preserves. The only true test is to smell and taste—if the fruit lacks full flavor, your results will disappoint. Slightly underripe to firm-ripe fruit is ideal. Overly ripe fruit can lead to problems with texture and spoilage. When the fruit you want is out of season, a wise choice is to buy unsweetened frozen fruits, which make excellent sweet preserves.

The recipes here call for fruits by weight because it is the most accurate measure. Frozen fruit, however, contains an excess of water and should be measured by volume after briefly thawing. Remove as little from the fruit as possible, peeling the skin when the recipe directs, and cutting away any bruised or unsound spots. In all the recipes, it is essential to rinse all fruits and remove all seeds before you begin.

Pectin

Pectin, found in the skin, seeds, and flesh of fruit, is a natural substance that reacts with sugar and acid to form a thick jell. Fruits are rated as having high or low pectin content (see *Pectin Content of Fruits, below*). High pectin content is crucial for the success of jellies, marmalades, and jellied fruit sauces. Pectin content is less important for softer-textured jams, conserves, and fruit butters.

Unfortunately, pectin can be fickle depending on climate and the variety and ripeness of the fruit. As fruit ripens, pectin breaks down, which is why barely ripe fruits are preferable. Prolonged cooking also deteriorates pectin, making it important not to exceed the recommended cooking times. When jelling is especially important—such as for jellies—we recommend testing for pectin, opposite. If your fruit does not have enough pectin for jelly, use commercial pectin and follow the package's directions.

An easy way to make firm preserves with a low-pectin fruit is to combine the fruit with an equal amount of grated tart apples. This will ensure that the apples cook quickly and thicken the preserves without influencing the flavor or texture of the dominant fruit.

COMMERCIAL PECTIN

We recommend using commercial pectin—a liquid or powdered substance derived primarily from citrus peels—only in jelly recipes with very low pectin fruits. Some recipes using commercial pectin require too much sugar for our tastes, and the high level of sugar can overwhelm the flavor of the fruit. Liquid and powdered pectin are not interchangeable in recipes. The order of combining and cooking ingredients depends on the type of pectin used.

PECTIN CONTENT OF FRUITS

Fruits should be barely ripe to firm-ripe.

High-Pectin Fruits: tart apples; crab apples; cranberries; currants; gooseberries; Eastern Concord, Muscadine, and Scuppernong grapes; lemons; loganberries; mayhaws; sour oranges; Damson and other tart plums (not Italian); quinces

Low-Pectin Fruits: apricots, blackberries, blueberries, cherries, elderberries, figs, all grapes but those listed above, huckleberries, guavas, nectarines, peaches, pears, pineapple, pomegranates, raspberries, rhubarb, sweet and Italian plums, and strawberries

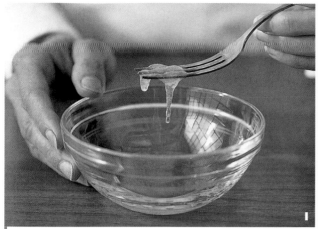

HOW TO TEST FOR PECTIN

Since pectin is essential for well-set jellies, we recommend testing fruit juice for pectin. There are two ways of determining the pectin content of the extracted juice. The first, the alcohol test, is closer to a scientific experiment, while the second involves making a small sample of jelly.

1 Alcohol Test: After extracting the juice from the fruit (refer to *Extracting the Juice, 66*), thoroughly blend 1 teaspoon cooled cooked juice with 1 tablespoon rubbing alcohol—do not taste! If a single gelatinous mass forms that can be picked up with a fork, there is ample pectin for jelly, marmalade, and jellied fruit sauces. Use ¾ to 1 cup sugar for 1 cup fruit or juice.

If the mixture separates into 2 or 3 masses, you can use ⅔ cup sugar. If numerous masses form, make preserves that do not need to jell, using half as much sugar as fruit or juice, or add commercial pectin to make jelled preserves. **Caution: The alcohol mixture is inedible; discard and do not taste!**

On rare occasions, inexplicably, a pectin-rich juice does not react with the alcohol, which is why the second test may be more practical.

2 Small Jelly Sample Test: After extracting the juice (refer to *Extracting the Juice, 66*), bring ⅓ cup of strained juice to a simmer in a small pan. Stir in ¼ cup sugar. Boil to the jelling point, 48, using the quick-chill test on 49. Adjust the pectin and lemon juice as needed, making calculations for the entire recipe. Add the remaining juice and proceed. When in doubt, use a little more sugar, adding fresh citrus juice to balance the sweetness.

Acid

Unlike pectin, the acid content of a fruit is easily determined by taste. If the fruit tastes as tart as a green apple, a sour plum, or rhubarb, there is sufficient acid to thicken the preserves, given the proper proportions of pectin and sugar. For fruits slightly less tart than these, such as sour cherries, elderberries, table grapes, and sweet plums, add ¼ tablespoon bottled lemon juice per cup of fruit or juice in the pan before cooking. For low-acid fruits, including sweet apples, sweet cherries, figs, nectarines, peaches, pears, and strawberries, add 1 tablespoon bottled lemon juice per cup. Alternatively, add orange juice to the uncooked fruit until it just barely begins to taste of orange. In addition to its role in helping preserves set, a few drops of lemon or orange juice perk up the flavor of the fruit. Keep in mind that underripe and just-ripe fruits are highest in acid. Citrus peel also enhances the flavor of sweet preserves, but it must be simmered in a small bit of water until tender before being added. Once tender, drain the peel, add it to the fruit, and save the pectin-rich simmering water to add to the preserves when possible.

Sugar and Other Sweeteners

The role of sugar goes beyond that of a sweetener in making jellies and jams. It preserves the fruit by inhibiting the development of bacteria. Decreasing the sugar in a recipe can drastically reduce shelf life. In addition, sugar reacts with the pectin to set jellies and jams. High-pectin fruits yield the best-set jellies but only in the presence of enough sugar. The more pectin in a mixture, the more sugar needed and the firmer the jelly.

It takes very little sugar to bring out a fruit's flavor. Finding the right amount of sugar is a balancing act. Less sugar means less preserves and they will keep for a shorter time, but the fruit flavors will be brighter. We recommend white sugar because its neutral taste does not compete with the flavors of the fresh fruit.

Sometimes jars of preserves end up with grainy crystals that multiply and ultimately solidify the contents. Prevent this by using a pastry brush dipped in water to dissolve any sugar clinging to the sides of the pan during cooking. If there is sugar on the sides of the pan when cooking is done, carefully remove it with a damp cloth before ladling out the preserves.

SWEETENING ALTERNATIVES

For a deeper, fuller flavor, substitute up to one-quarter of the sugar in a recipe with brown sugar. Alternatively, up to half the sugar in any recipe without commercial pectin may be replaced with mild honey. Some manufacturers of commerical pectin allow the substitution of sugar with up to one-quarter light corn syrup. Keep in mind that honey is sweeter and stronger flavored than sugar. Corn syrup is also very sweet, but is neutral tasting. Another alternative is fruit juice. Apple juice is a favorite because of its relatively neutral flavor and high pectin content.

SUGAR SUBSTITUTES

Nonnutritive sweeteners work only in thick jams and fruit butters, which don't rely on the sugar's interaction with pectin to set. Keep in mind that anything made with any sort of nonnutritive sweetener will lack the preserving power of sugar and will need to be processed in a water bath for 15 minutes. Follow the manufacturer's directions on substituting for sugar.

Equipment

As with any craft, the right tools make the job easy and give you a running jump on success. In addition to standard cutting, measuring, and mixing equipment, we recommend the following:

Essential: The most important tool is a heavy, broad, shallow 7- to 8-quart saucepan. Heavy-duty nonstick versions work well, but any nonreactive surface is fine. Stay away from uncoated aluminum, copper, iron, thin enamel, or anything galvanized.

Long-handled Utensils: A broad wooden spoon, a large stainless-steel spoon, a whisk, a skimmer, and a 4- to 8-ounce ladle (preferably with a spout).

A 1-inch-wide pastry brush with natural bristles, to wash down sugar crystals.

A fine-mesh strainer, a colander, a ruler, a timer, and a jar funnel.

To Can Jars: A large, broad, deep pot for a boiling-water canner, canning jars without nicks or cracks, metal rings and new lids (shown 12), and a jar lifter (shown 14).

For Jelly: A jelly bag (shown 67) is preferable for straining juice for jelly. However, cotton string and 18-inch squares of flannel or unbleached muslin, or 4 layers of cheesecloth may be used alternatively.

For Microwave Cooking: A 2-quart, heat-resistant glass, liquid measuring pitcher.

Helpful: A food processor, a kitchen scale (10-pound capacity), a candy thermometer, a food mill, a potato masher or a large pestle, a cherry pitter, a citrus juicer, and a zester.

Jelled Preserves

Sweet preserves fall loosely into two categories—those that are meant to jell and those that aren't. Jelled preserves include jellies, marmalades, jams, and some preserves. While they range from firm to soft and almost runny, they are all based on the principle of boiling sweetened fruit or juice until enough moisture has evaporated and pectin, acid, and sugar have concentrated. This point is referred to as the jelling point and is best reached by rapid boiling, because the elements that make preserves jell—pectin, sugar, and acid—interact most effectively over intense heat (prolonged cooking deteriorates the pectin). Rapid boiling also tends to keep jellies clearer than slow-cooked ones, while retaining the flavor of fresh fruit.

This is small-batch preserving. Do not double the amounts in recipes. Doubled recipes do not always jell properly.

BOILING PRESERVES

Choose a large, broad, heavy pan. We recommend cooking the fruit in batches of 2 to 2½ pounds or less per pan. Cook the preserves rapidly over high heat to retain the flavor and pectin of the fruit. Preserves tend to foam dramatically when boiled. Any additive, such as honey, will cause even more foam. For clear jellies, skim the foam throughout the cooking process.

THE JELLING POINT

This is the moment of truth when everything comes together and when, once cooled, the preserves will jell. The jelling point is unpredictable, so it is a good idea to start testing for it early and often while cooking, opposite. A good visual indicator is when, after boiling high and foamy in the pan, the mixture settles, and suddenly its surface is covered with furiously boiling small bubbles.

HOW TO TEST
FOR THE JELLING POINT

There are three reliable tests for the jelling point: the spoon test, the temperature test, and the quick-chill test. They are best used in conjunction with one another, especially if you are making jam or jelly for the first time. Most experienced preserves makers, however, come to rely on just one test, as well as their eyes and nose. Whichever you choose, be certain the mixture has reached the consistency you want before you declare it ready.

1 Spoon Test: This test works best for jellies but is also effective for all but the thickest purees. Scoop up a little boiling syrup or some of the thinnest part of the fruit mixture with a cool, dry stainless-steel spoon. Raise it over the pan, but out of the steam, then turn it so that the syrup falls back into the pan off the spoon's side. At first, the drip will be light and syrupy. As it continues to cook and the syrup thickens, 2 large drops will form along the spoon's edge. When the drips slide together and fall as one, jelling has begun. For a tender-firm set, wait until these drops are heavy. When the drips glide together and hang off the edge of the spoon a moment before dropping, the sheeting stage has been reached, and this will make as firm a jell as the pectin can give.

2 Temperature Test: We use temperature as an indication the jelling point is near, then finish with the quick-chill test. Use a candy thermometer. Traditionally, the jelling point is 8 to 10 degrees higher than the boiling point of water, which is 212°F. So, at sea level, the jelling point is 220°F to

222°F. (For higher elevations, see *High-Altitude Preserving, 50.*) These temperatures are based on ¾ cup sugar for each 1 cup fruit and result in a moderately firm jell. For a very soft jell, stop cooking at 2 to 3 degrees lower. For a very firm jell, boil to 3 to 4 degrees higher.

3 Quick-Chill Test: This is the surest test because you actually see how the finished product will jell, but it is a bit more involved. We recommend using the temperature or spoon test as an indication of progress, and then, as the preserves begin to settle, try the quick-chill test. Before you start cooking, place a couple of saucers in the freezer or set a small metal bowl in a larger bowl of ice water. Remove the pan from the heat each time you do this test, or the preserves could overcook. Drop a small amount of syrup onto an icy saucer and return it to the freezer— or drop the sample into the icy bowl. After about 3 minutes, pull a finger through the center of the chilled preserves. For a soft set, the 2 sides should glide back together slowly. For a tender-firm set, the 2 sides should not move and the surface should wrinkle when gently pushed.

Once the desired consistency has been reached, remove the pan from the heat. Undercooked preserves can be cooked again until set—you can remove the pan from the heat as many times as necessary and quality will not be affected— but overcooked preserves are usually lost. All jelled preserves will be thicker after cooling and will continue to set for 1 to 3 weeks after being made.

Putting Up Preserves

There are three ways of keeping your homemade preserves. Based on how long you want to keep your preserves, choose from among refrigeration, freezing, and canning.

REFRIGERATION

This is the simplest method, but also the most limited. Once cooked, pour the hot preserves into sterilized jars, 12, cover, and refrigerate, placing them where temperature changes from opening the refrigerator door won't affect them. The shelf life of refrigerated preserves depends on the amount of sugar in the recipe—preserves made with one-half to two-thirds as much sugar as fruit will keep in the refrigerator for at least 2 to 3 weeks. Those made with equal amounts of sugar and fruit will last for 2 months or more.

FREEZING

Jelled preserves do not freeze well. All other preserves will last for 6 months when frozen in freezer containers. Leave ½-inch headspace in containers, 12. Leave the same headspace in freezer bags, but force out the air. Label with the contents and date frozen.

CANNING

Please read the directions for safe and proper canning, 8 to 19, before proceeding. The best method for storing preserves is to pour them into small jars outfitted with new flat lids and metal rings, leaving ¼-inch headspace, 12, unless other- wise noted in the recipe, and to process them in a boiling-water canner, 14, for 5 to 15 minutes, according to the recipe.

We generally call for half-pint jars, which should be free of nicks or cracks. While the jars and metal rings can be reused, use new flat lids each time. See Equipment, 11. Wash in hot, soapy water and rinse well.

Preserves that will be processed for less than 10 minutes, such as jellies, must go into sterilized jars. To sterilize the jars, lower them into the canning kettle filled with hot water. Be sure they are all covered and filled with water, and boil for 10 minutes at altitudes of 1,000 feet or less (at higher altitudes, boil 1 additional minute for each 1,000 feet); include the canning ladle if you are using one. Leave the jars in the kettle until needed. Place the lids and metal rings nearby in a bowl of very hot water to soften the gummy seal. Do not boil them or you may ruin the seal. While the jelly is boiling, lift out the sterilized jars, pouring the hot water back into the pan, and stand the jars upright on a clean dish towel. See Packing Jars, 12.

Ladle or pour the hot preserves into the hot jars, leaving a ¼-inch headspace, 12, unless otherwise noted in the recipe. Wipe the rims clean with a clean dish towel and set on the lids. Screw on the rings and, using the jar lifter, lower the jars into the kettle filled with hot water. Be sure the water covers the lids and boil in the boiling-water canner for the time directed. See Processing Canned Foods, 14. Carefully remove the jars again with the jar lifter and set them on a clean towel to cool. See Cooling the Jars, 16. When a seal is formed and the jar is cool, write the name of the preserves and the date on the lid with a permanent marker. See Storing Canned Goods, 17.

SPOILAGE

Discard preserves that exhibit any of the following: mold (rare in unopened canned preserves, inevit- able at some point in refrigerated preserves), fermentation, or bub- bling. See Checking for Spoilage, and Handling Contaminated Food and Jars, 19.

Once opened, all preserves need to be refrigerated. To prevent mold from developing, use a clean, moist dish towel to wipe off any residue above the level of the preserves.

HIGH-ALTITUDE PRESERVING

Reduced jelling-point temperatures:

1,000 feet	218°F to 220°F
2,000 feet	216°F to 218°F
3,000 feet	214°F to 216°F
4,000 feet	212°F to 214°F
5,000 feet	211°F to 212°F
6,000 feet	209°F to 211°F
7,000 feet	207°F to 209°F
8,000 feet	205°F to 207°F

Increased processing times:
1,001–6,000 feet, add 5 minutes
6,001+ feet, add 10 minutes

Making and Cooking Jam

Jam contains lightly jelled whole, crushed, or ground fruit. It is the simplest and most forgiving of sweet preserves to make—there is lots of leeway in consistency and most fruits need little preparation. Use firm-ripe fruit sliced or chopped ¼ to ½ inch thick, unless otherwise noted.

Please read the directions for safe and proper canning, 8 to 19, before proceeding. Ladle the jam into hot small jars, leaving ¼-inch headspace, 12, and process jam in a boiling-water canner for 10 minutes, 14.

Five Fruits Jam Cockaigne

About nine ½-pint jars

Stem, hull, or pit as necessary, placing each fruit in its own bowl:

1 pound strawberries
1½ pounds red currants
1 pound sweet cherries
1 pound gooseberries
1 pound red raspberries

Put strawberries in one pan, currants and cherries in another, and gooseberries and raspberries in a third pan. Lightly crush all but the gooseberries and raspberries. Measure:

7 cups sugar

Mix 1 cup of the sugar with the strawberries and 3 cups of sugar with the fruits in each of the remaining pans. Bring each jam to a boil, stirring frequently. Cook to the jelling point, 48.

Remove from the heat and skim off any foam. Combine the jams before ladling into hot jars. See *Putting Up Preserves*, 50. Leave ¼-inch headspace, 12, and process for 10 minutes, 14. (Photo, opposite.)

Berry Jam

About five ½-pint jars

Peel, core, and finely grate:

8 ounces tart green apples

Mix with:

2 pounds blackberries, blueberries, cranberries, elderberries, or raspberries, stemmed
1 tablespoon orange juice
3 cups sugar

Cook, crushing one-quarter of the berries in the pan (but do not crush raspberries). Boil rapidly, stirring frequently, to the jelling point, 48. Remove from the heat and skim off any foam before ladling into hot jars. See *Putting Up Preserves*, 50. Leave ¼-inch headspace, 12, and process for 10 minutes, 14.

STRAWBERRY JAM

About three ½-pint jars

A popular jam with good texture.
Prepare the recipe for *Berry Jam, left,* using hulled strawberries and substituting ¼ cup bottled lemon juice for the apples. Reduce the sugar to 2½ cups.

GOOSEBERRY JAM

About three ½-pint jars

Prepare the recipe for *Berry Jam, left,* omitting the apples and substituting 2 pounds gooseberries for the berries. If available, cook each batch with 6 elderflowers tied in a cloth. Squeeze their syrup into the jam, then discard the flowers.

CURRANTS

Currants are scarce in this country, but can be found from mid-June through August. Red and black currants are different species. The red are juicy, with a brilliant fruity sharpness. Black currants are larger than red—over ½ inch in diameter. They are not quite as juicy, and their flavor is muted. Yellow currants might be a variety of black or a native berry. Pink currants are a variant of red. There are opalescent white currants, which may have come from either the red or the black species. Light-colored fruits are less acidic and are translucent when cooked. Currants are very high in pectin, a soluble fiber.

Seedless Red Grape Jam

About five ½-pint jars

This jam is a boon for those outside Concord and Muscadine country.
Stem:
3 pounds Flame seedless grapes
Mix with:
2½ cups sugar
Steep, 59. Strain the grape syrup into a large saucepan, reserving the grapes.
Add to the pan:
¼ cup bottled lemon juice
Slowly bring the syrup to a boil, then boil rapidly until it falls from a spoon in 2 heavy drops. Stir in the grapes. Boil rapidly to the jelling point, 48. Remove from the heat and skim off any foam before ladling into hot jars. See *Putting Up Preserves*, 50. Leave ¼-inch headspace, 12, and process for 10 minutes, 14.

Plum Jam

About four ½-pint jars

Juicy Greengages, Damsons, Mirabelles, and many wild plums make excellent jam. Leave the peel on for maximum flavor and nutrients.
Stem, halve, and pit:
2 pounds plums
Halve large plums once more.
Mix with:
2½ cups sugar
¼ cup bottled lemon juice
Cook, lightly crushing some of the fruit. Boil rapidly, stirring frequently, to the jelling point, 48. Remove from the heat and skim off any foam before ladling into hot jars. See *Putting Up Preserves*, 50. Leave ¼-inch headspace, 12, and process for 10 minutes, 14.

PLUMS

While there are only two or three species of peaches or apricots, there are sixteen or more species of plums. Wild purple, red, or yellow American plums, such as Beach, Sand, Sierra, and Wild Goose make superbly tart sauces, jams, and jellies. European plums include astringent blue Damsons, golden Greengages, and small yellow Mirabelles, incomparable for preserves.

Naturally Sweetened Pear and Grape Jam

About three ½-pint jars

You must use high-pectin grapes (Eastern Concord, Muscadine, and Scuppernog) in this recipe.
6 pounds high-pectin grapes (see note), preferably dark-skinned
Mash while bringing to a simmer. Remove from the heat and strain through a sieve into a bowl, pressing out all the juice. Boil down to 3 cups, skimming. Core and cut in 1-inch-wide slices:
2 pounds pears
Add the pears to the juice in the saucepan. Simmer until the pears are tender, about 15 minutes, stirring frequently. Boil rapidly to the jelling point, 48. Remove from the heat and skim off any foam before ladling into hot jars. See *Putting Up Preserves*, 50. Leave ¼-inch headspace, 12, and process for 10 minutes, 14.

Golden Cherry Tomato and Ginger Jam

About three ½-pint jars

These golden preserves (above) are almost tropical. Serve as a condiment or jam.

Slice in half, catching the juice:

2 pounds yellow or orange cherry tomatoes or plum tomatoes

(Quarter plum tomatoes.)
Combine with:

2 cups sugar

Steep, 59. Peel and slice in thin strips:

¼ pound fresh ginger

Finely grate the zest and extract the juice of:

½ pound lemons

Strain the tomato syrup into a large saucepan, reserving the tomatoes. Mix the ginger, lemon zest, and lemon juice with the tomatoes. Slowly bring the syrup to a boil, then boil rapidly until it falls from a spoon in 2 heavy drops. Blend in the tomato mixture.

Boil rapidly to the jelling point, 48. Remove from the heat and skim off any foam before ladling into hot jars. See *Putting Up Preserves*, 50. Leave ¼-inch headspace, 12, and process for 10 minutes, 14.

GINGER

Mistakenly called a root, ginger is a tropical rhizome that is thought to be native to Southeast Asia. When buying, select the hardest, heaviest rhizomes. Check where the knobs have been broken: the longer the rhizome has grown before harvesting, the more fibrous it becomes, and the more fibers you will see at the break. Mature fresh ginger is hotter and to some extent more flavorful.

Microwave Naturally Sweetened Apple Jam

About two ½-pint jars

This easy jam (opposite) has plenty of texture and flavor and no added sugar. Peel, core, and finely grate or chop in a food processor:

1¼ pounds cooking apples

Mix together thoroughly in a 2-quart microwave-safe container with:

2 cups thawed frozen unsweetened apple juice concentrate

Cover with wax paper, place in the microwave, and bring to a boil on high. Stir, then cook until the apples are soft. Stir in:

1 teaspoon ground cinnamon
¼ teaspoon ground cloves
¼ teaspoon ground nutmeg

Cover and cook on high until thick, stirring and checking the consistency every 3 minutes. Remove from the microwave and skim off any foam. Stir in:

1 teaspoon grated orange zest

Ladle into hot jars. See *Putting Up Preserves*, 50. Leave ¼-inch headspace, 12, and process for 15 minutes, 14.

Microwave Strawberry Rhubarb Jam

About three ½-pint jars

Hull:

1 pound strawberries

Chop finely with:

6 ounces tender red rhubarb stalks

Mix together thoroughly in a 2-quart microwave-safe container with:

2½ teaspoons orange juice
2 teaspoons bottled lemon juice
¼ cup powdered pectin, 44

Cover with wax paper, place in the microwave, and bring to a boil on high. Stir, then cook until the strawberries and rhubarb are soft.

Stir in:

1 cup plus 3 tablespoons sugar

Stir until the sugar dissolves, then cover and cook on high. Test for the jelling point, 48, after the jam comes to a boil, then every 30 seconds until the desired consistency. Remove from the microwave and skim off any foam before ladling into hot jars. See *Putting Up Preserves*, 50. Leave ¼-inch headspace, 12, and process for 10 minutes, 14.

> ### MICROWAVE PEACH OR NECTARINE JAM
>
> *Capture the perfume of summer-ripened fruits in this easy jam. It's a breeze to make.*
>
> Prepare the recipe for *Microwave Strawberry Rhubarb Jam, left,* substituting 1⅔ pounds finely chopped firm-ripe fruits (fuzz removed by gently rubbing with a damp cloth if using peaches) for the strawberries and rhubarb.

Making and Cooking Preserves

Some confusion swirls around the definition of preserves. We use the term to refer to the category of foods described in this entire chapter—jams, jellies, marmalades, conserves, preserves, and jellied fruit sauces. To be more exact, preserves are defined as fruit in syrup that is only slightly jelled. Similar to jam, preserves are chunkier and found in two styles. In one, the fruit is close together in a heavy syrup and thick enough to spread. In the other, more European style, the fruit is loose in a light syrup. These preserves may drip off the toast, but their flavor is very

fresh. Runny preserves are perfect for spooning over pancakes and waffles, ice cream, yogurts, puddings, and even cakes.

Whichever style you choose, use your finest fruits to make preserves. Fruits for preserves can be just ripe to fully ripe, since jelling is less important.

STEEPING AND PLUMPING

Because of their unique texture, preserves benefit from both **steeping** and **plumping** before canning. Gently mix the raw fruit and sugar in a nonreactive bowl until all the

sugar has liquefied, cover the fruit mixture, and let **steep** in a cool place for 4 to 8 hours (or in the refrigerator for up to 24 hours).

Cook the preserves as outlined in *Boiling Preserves*, 48. You may can the preserves as soon as they reach the jelling point, 48, or pour them into a shallow dish, cover loosely and set them in a cool place to **plump** overnight. Plumping is optional, but we recommend this step to ensure tender fruit that will not float in the syrup in the jars. The next day, return the preserves to a rolling boil before canning.

Strawberry Preserves

About four ½-pint jars

Hull:
2 pounds firm-ripe strawberries, crush half if desired
Gently mix with:
3 cups sugar

Steep, above. Stir in:
¼ cup bottled lemon juice
Boil rapidly, stirring frequently, to the jelling point, 48. Remove from the heat and skim off any foam.

Plump overnight, above. Return the preserves to a boil before ladling into hot jars. See *Putting Up Preserves*, 50. Leave ¼-inch headspace, 12, and process for 10 minutes, 14.

Apricot Preserves

About six ½-pint jars

Pull apart on the seam line:
5 pounds unpeeled sweet firm-ripe apricots
Gently mix with:
6 cups sugar
Steep, above. Stir into the apricots:
¼ cup bottled lemon juice
¼ cup orange juice
Cook in 2 batches. Boil rapidly,

stirring frequently, to the jelling point, 48. Remove from the heat and skim off any foam. Combine the batches and plump overnight, above. Return the preserves to a boil before ladling into hot jars. See *Putting Up Preserves*, 50. Leave ¼-inch headspace, 12, and process for 10 minutes, 14.

PEACH OR NECTARINE PRESERVES

Use the tastiest fruit you can find. Prepare the recipe for *Apricot Preserves, left*, substituting peaches or nectarines for the apricots. After removing any fuzz by gently rubbing with a damp cloth, slice ¼ inch thick and prepare the fruit as you would the apricots.

From left: Apricot Preserves, Strawberry Preserves

Mango Preserves

About nine ½-pint jars

Luscious when mangoes are ripe, both on toast and as a relish for chicken and fish (opposite, middle). When mangoes are less flavorful, make Chili Mango Preserves, right.
Peel:

6½ pounds firm-ripe mangoes

Cut the flesh off the seed in ½-inch-wide slices, then cut the slices crosswise in half. Gently mix with:

6 cups sugar

Steep, 59. Stir in:

½ cup bottled lemon juice
1½ tablespoons grated orange zest

Cook in 2 batches. Boil rapidly, stirring frequently, to the jelling point, 48. Remove from the heat and skim off any foam. Combine the batches and plump overnight, 59. Return the preserves to a boil before ladling into hot jars. See *Putting Up Preserves*, 50. Leave ¼-inch headspace, 12, and process for 10 minutes, 14.

> **CHILI MANGO PRESERVES**
>
> *About ten ½-pint jars*
>
> Char (as for roast peppers, 41), peel, seed, and cut into small dice 1 pound dried, mild chiles, preferably pasilla. Simmer with ½ cup lime juice until softened, about 2 minutes. Add 1½ tablespoons red pepper flakes (or to taste) and ½ teaspoon salt. Mix into hot *Mango Preserves, left*.

Fig Preserves

About four ½-pint jars

Excellent as a glaze for red meats (opposite, top). If their skins are tough, cover the figs with boiling water and let stand for 10 minutes, then proceed.
Stem and quarter lengthwise:

2 pounds firm-ripe figs

Gently mix with:

2 cups packed light brown sugar

Steep, 59. Stir in:

¼ cup thawed frozen unsweetened apple juice concentrate

Simmer until the fig peel is soft, 25 to 30 minutes. Stir in:

¼ cup bottled lemon juice
2 tablespoons orange juice

Boil rapidly, stirring frequently, to the jelling point, 48. Remove from the heat and skim off any foam. Stir in:

⅛ teaspoon ground cinnamon

Plump overnight, 59. Return the preserves to a boil before ladling into hot jars. See *Putting Up Preserves*, 50. Leave ¼-inch headspace, 12, and process for 10 minutes, 14.

Rose Hip and Tangerine Spoon Sweet

About one ½-pint jar

An exceptional traditional Greek preserve (opposite, bottom).
Combine in a small, heavy saucepan:

5 tablespoons water
2½ tablespoons sugar

Stir over low heat until the sugar dissolves, then cover and simmer for 2 minutes. Slice off the stems and blossom threads, then peel off any frost-browned skin from:

Fourteen 1-inch unsprayed ripe orange or red rose hips, or 28 small ones

Quarter large hips; halve small hips. Scrape out the seeds and any hard linings. You'll need ⅔ cup rose hips. Add to the syrup, cover, and simmer for 5 minutes, then turn into a bowl. Combine in the same, unrinsed pan:

⅓ cup peeled, seeded, and chopped sweet tangerines or oranges
⅓ cup water

Simmer until tender, about 4 minutes. Add the rose hips and:

⅔ cup sugar
¼ cup apple juice
1 tablespoon bottled lemon juice

Boil gently to the jelling point, 48, washing down the sides of the pan with a wet pastry brush to remove any sugar crystals. Remove from the heat and skim off any foam. Plump overnight, 59. Bring to a boil and pour into a hot, sterilized jar. Cover and refrigerate.

Making and Cooking Conserves

Conserves resemble thicker preserves in consistency but, rather than spread them, you eat conserves with a fork or spoon. They often contain a mixture of fruits, usually one citrus, and special touches like raisins, nuts, or ginger. Conserves cross between sweet and savory and can be served as a condiment for poultry and meat or stirred into softened ice cream.

Because conserves are dense with rich ingredients that easily scorch,

most are simmered over low heat to the jelling point, 48, or until thick. Stir these mixtures carefully, especially toward the end. After adding the sugar, it is important to stir and simmer until the sugar has completely dissolved. To test for the jelling point, use the quick-chill test, 49, when the mixture has become noticeably thick. If the fruit is cooked yet the syrup is too thin, remove the fruit with a slotted spoon, set it aside, and simmer the

syrup to the desired thickness. When the syrup reaches the jelling point, remove the pan from the heat immediately and return the fruit to the syrup.

Please read the directions for safe and proper canning, 8 to 19, before proceeding. Pack the hot fruit into hot jars, leaving ¼-inch headspace, 12. Process in a boiling-water canner for 15 minutes, 14.

Peach Conserves

About eight ½-pint jars

A rich accompaniment (opposite) for dark meats and spicy dishes.
Remove the zest with a peeler, then chop the zest and peeled pulp of:
1 large orange
1 small lemon
Peel or remove the fuzz by gently wiping with a damp cloth, then pit and cut in 1-inch-size chunks:
3 pounds firm-ripe peaches
Gently mix all the fruits in a large, heavy saucepan. Stir in:
8 ounces golden raisins

3½ cups sugar
Bring to a boil, reduce the heat, and simmer, stirring frequently, until thick, about 1 hour. Toast, then stir in:
4 ounces pecan pieces
Cook for 5 minutes. Remove from the heat and add:
¼ cup bourbon
Ladle the hot conserves into hot jars. See *Putting Up Preserves*, 50. Leave ¼-inch headspace, 12, and process for 15 minutes, 14.

> ### BLUE PLUM CONSERVES
> *About nine ½-pint jars*
> *Serve alongside white meats and poultry.*
> Prepare the recipe for *Peach Conserves, left,* using 3 pounds blue (or any) plums, 10 ounces dark raisins, 3¾ cups sugar, walnuts instead of pecans, and brandy in place of bourbon. Simmering time is about 1¼ hours.

Cranberry Conserves

About six ½-pint jars

Chill, cut in half lengthwise, and then slice very thinly, removing any seeds:
12 ounces unpeeled oranges
Place with their juice in a small skillet with:
½ cup apple cider
Cover and simmer until the orange peel is soft, 15 to 20 minutes. Peel,

core, and cut into ½-inch chunks to make 1½ cups:
1 pound fresh pineapple
Pick over:
1 pound cranberries
Combine all fruits in a large saucepan with:
4 cups sugar
½ cup bottled lemon juice

1 teaspoon ground cinnamon
½ teaspoon whole cloves
Bring to a boil, reduce the heat, and simmer, stirring frequently, until thick, about 45 minutes. Ladle the hot conserves into hot jars. See *Putting Up Preserves*, 50. Leave ¼-inch headspace, 12, and process for 15 minutes, 14.

Christmas Conserves

About nine ½-pint jars

Make these colorful conserves (opposite) with fruits of the holiday season.
Chill, cut into quarters, then slice very thinly, removing any seeds:

12 ounces unpeeled oranges

Chill and slice in the thinnest possible rounds:

12 ounces unpeeled limes

Cut in half lengthwise, ignoring seeds (they will cook tender):

12 ounces kumquats

Cover the fruits with cold water in a saucepan and simmer, covered, until the citrus peel is soft, about 15 minutes.
Measure, then divide in half:

6 cups sugar

Drain the citrus fruit mixture and combine with 3 cups of the sugar in a saucepan. Rapidly boil until the slices are translucent and the mixture is thick, about 35 minutes. While the citrus fruit is cooking, peel, quarter, core, and slice lengthwise ½-inch thick, dropping the pieces into cold water to keep from darkening:

12 ounces tart apples

12 ounces firm-ripe pears

12 ounces ripe quinces (if unavailable, use 1¼ pounds apples and 1 pound pears total)

Mix the remaining 3 cups of sugar in a large, heavy saucepan with:

5 cups water

Stir over low heat until the sugar dissolves, then cover and bring the syrup to a simmer. Drain the apple mixture and add it to the syrup. Simmer for 15 minutes.
Combine both pans and mix in:

12 ounces cranberries

Return to a boil. Remove from the heat, cover for 5 minutes and then stir. Ladle the hot conserves into hot jars. See *Putting Up Preserves*, 50. Leave ¼-inch headspace, 12, and process for 15 minutes, 14.

Rhubarb Conserves

About five ½-pint jars

Serve these spicy, tart conserves slightly warmed with rich poultry or meat.
Chill, then slice very thinly, removing any seeds:

8 ounces unpeeled oranges

4 ounces unpeeled lemons

Peel, then cut in slivers:

1 ounce fresh ginger

Combine citrus with its juice and ginger in a small pan with:

1 cup apple cider

Cover and simmer until the citrus peel is soft, about 15 minutes. Cut into inch-size pieces:

1 pound slender red rhubarb

Combine citrus, ginger, and rhubarb in a large, heavy saucepan with:

½ cup golden raisins

½ teaspoon ground cinnamon

¼ teaspoon ground mace

3¼ cups sugar

Bring to a boil, reduce the heat, and simmer, stirring frequently, until thick, about 40 minutes. (The conserves will thicken further once cool.) Ladle the hot conserves into hot jars. See *Putting Up Preserves*, 50. Leave ¼-inch headspace, 12, and process for 15 minutes, 14.

KUMQUATS

The size of a bird's egg, this fruit is unique among citrus and is actually in a different genus. Kumquats' one-bite size also makes them unique. The kumquat for eating fresh, rind and all, is Meiwa. It is round with sweet, spicy flesh and rind. Nagami, the other kumquat that comes to market, is oblong. Nagami's rind is sweet, but its flesh is sour, which is a pleasing combination for preserves and marmalades. Both types vary in color from gold to orange. Kumquats are available in early winter, and the freshest supply may well be at an Asian market. Select fruits that are thoroughly plump, not shriveled at either end. For eating, just rinse well; the small seeds should not be a problem. In fruit salads and compotes, if the fruits are small enough, leave them whole; otherwise, slice lengthwise in half.

QUINCES

To fill a room with sweet, rich fragrance, place a ripe gold quince in the middle of it. A member of the rose family, a quince looks like a fat and lumpy pear. Probably because they are too astringent to eat raw, quinces have fallen out of favor in this country. But when slices are poached until translucent and a deep shade of red, their flavor is reminiscent of rose and apple, with a touch of pineapple in the variety called Pineapple quince. Quinces are available in October and November.

Select fruits with some fragrance, although they will ripen nicely at room temperature. Avoid those with spots, bruises, and tiny holes. Handle gently, for these seemingly sturdy fruits bruise easily.

To prepare, rub off any fuzz. Peel with a vegetable peeler, and use a chef's knife to cut the fruit in half and then in quarters. With a paring knife, trim out the core, dipping down to remove all the white grains. Quinces cook just like apples except they can take up to twice the cooking time.

Making Jelly

Many consider jelly-making to be the highest form of preserving fruit. A good jelly is a bright, clear, tender-set jell made from strained fruit juice, wine, spirits, or even herb infusions. Two cooking processes are involved. First, juice is extracted from nearly every part of the fruit. Then, after the juice has settled overnight, it is boiled with sugar until firm enough to hold its shape when cold. Picture-perfect jelly takes time to make and is more dependent on just the right proportions of pectin, sugar, and acid than any other type of preserves.

PREPARING THE FRUIT

When selecting fruits for jelly, mix one-quarter slightly underripe to firm-ripe for pectin and three-quarters firm-ripe for flavor. With medium- and low-pectin fruits, 44, pectin must be added anyway, so use fully ripe fruit for the deepest flavor. Chop hard fruits such as apples into small (¼-inch) bits and mash soft fruits. Skins, cores, and seeds are not removed because they contribute pectin and/or flavor and will be strained out in the end. Thick stems are the only parts to trim away.

EXTRACTING THE JUICE

Place the prepared fruit in a large, broad, heavy, shallow saucepan—the wider it is, the more efficiently the fruit will cook. Water may be necessary to prevent scorching, or to produce juice from firm fruits, such as apples and quinces, but add only as much as needed. When a recipe says "cover" with water, just barely cover—never float—the fruit. Cover the pan and bring to a boil over high heat, lifting the lid and mashing and stirring frequently (**1**). Turn down the heat and simmer until the fruit is thoroughly soft, frequently stirring and crushing. To preserve pectin, do not boil rapidly and do not cook longer than called for in the recipe.

To strain the juice from the fruit, we recommend you use a ready-made jelly bag (**2**), which consists of a three-prong steel frame fitted with a cloth or nylon sack. Some models come with a shallow bowl that hooks onto the frame under the sack. Replace or wash the jelly bags after every use, according to the manufacturer's instructions.

If you do not own a jelly bag, use the following method: Wet and wring out 4 layers of cheesecloth. Lay the cloth in a colander set inside a deep bowl and ladle or pour in the contents of the pan (**3**). The bag or colander (**4**) can be left to drip for up to 12 hours, but 3 to 4 hours is adequate—rarely more than a spoonful of juice will come after that. For clear jelly, do not squeeze the bag or press the fruit against the cheesecloth. For maximum yield but cloudy and possibly bitter jelly, squeeze out all the juice. When the dripping stops, you can gently press the bag to flatten it, and pulp in the center will drip. For the clearest jelly, strain the juice a second time, using a fresh wet cloth, and do not squeeze.

All the juice for a jelly must be cloth strained, including any added citrus juices. Line a small strainer with a moist cloth and pour the juices through it into the pan.

After straining, all juices profit from settling. Pour into a glass container and let stand undisturbed in the refrigerator. After 12 to 24 hours, carefully pour off the clear juice (discard the sediment). This settling is essential for grape juice, to remove tartrate crystals that might form later in the jar. The juice may now be frozen or canned to use at a more convenient time.

VARYING FRUIT JUICE YIELDS

Occasionally, a fruit will yield much less juice than expected, usually because the fruit was dry. (This can happen with apples.) If your juice is very thick, blend in enough water until it has the consistency and taste of a natural juice. If the juice is not thick, return the fruit pulp to a pan with some water and repeat the cooking and straining steps.

Cooking Jelly

Please read the directions for safe and Proper canning, 8 to 19, and *Making Jelly*, 66, before proceeding. Yield for jelly generally equals the amount of strained fruit juice. Have a thermometer and chilled saucers on hand for the quick-chill test, 49. Measure the juice into a heavy, shallow saucepan. The syrup will boil up high, so use a pan at least 4 times taller than the syrup is deep. Bring the juice to a simmer over high heat. Remove the pan from the heat. Add the sugar (**1**) and any lemon juice called for and mix thoroughly. Use a wet pastry brush to wash down any sugar from the sides of the pan (**2**). Return the pan to the heat and boil rapidly, stirring constantly. When the syrup thickens noticeably, start testing for a jell, 49 (**3**). If a skin forms while the pan is off the heat waiting for the quick-chill test, whisk to break up and blend it back in. When the syrup reaches the jelling point, remove from the heat immediately, and then skim off any foam.

Pour the hot jelly into hot, sterilized ½-pint jars, leaving ¼-inch headspace, 12. Process jellies in a boiling-water canner for 5 minutes, 14. Jellies may be refrigerated, but they do not freeze well.

DECORATIVE TOUCHES

A large bay leaf; a curl of citrus zest; a cinnamon stick; a spray of rose hips; a sprig of herb; a dried red chili pod—one of these set in the jar before the hot jelly is poured in lifts the jelly from special to superb. Choose garnishes whose flavors blend well with the jelly. If the garnish floats, occasionally turn the jar gently, once it has sealed and thoroughly cooled, until the object is where you want it.

TROUBLESHOOTING

If the canned jelly is too soft, remember that some mixtures do not fully set for 2 weeks. You can set the jars in full sun for 3 weeks, and the jelly may set softly. Refrigerate for more firmness. Alternatively, the surest way of setting runny jelly is to boil it again with 1 tablespoon sugar, 1 tablespoon water, and 1 teaspoon powdered pectin for each cup of jelly—cook no more than 1 quart at a time. Bring the pectin mixture to a boil over high heat, stirring constantly. Add the melted jelly, bring to a full boil, and boil for just 30 seconds, stirring constantly. Remove from the heat, skim off any foam, and pour into sterilized jars. Or, the easiest of all, label runny jelly as syrup and use as a topping or meat glaze.

JELLY BAG BUTTER

If, after dripping, the pulp in the bag is still flavorful and not too thick with seeds or tough bits of peel, put it in a heavy, shallow pan, stir in apple juice until the pulp is the consistency of applesauce, and simmer, stirring frequently, until thick. Put through a food mill, then return to the heat and sweeten to taste with sugar, brown sugar, or honey. Simmer down to fruit butter thickness, adding a few sweet spices, if desired. See *Microwave Honey Butter*, 82.

WILDERMUTH

Pure Blackberry Jelly

About three ½-pint jars

*Almost any sort of wild berry works
for this jelly (above), but boysenberries,
loganberries, marion berries, and olallie-
berries work especially well. One form
of blackberry or another is in season
from June through mid-September.
No water is added to this pure berry
jelly, and there is just enough sugar to
firm it up.*

Refer to *Making Jelly*, 66.

Thoroughly crush in a large, heavy
saucepan:

4 pounds blackberries

Cover, bring to a boil, then reduce
the heat and simmer until soupy,
about 10 minutes, mashing frequently.
Strain, 66. Transfer the juice to a
glass container and refrigerate until
the sediment has settled. Pour the
clear juice into a measuring cup,
leaving the sediment behind. For
each cup juice, add:

¾ cup sugar

Boil rapidly, stirring frequently, to
the jelling point, 48. Remove from
the heat and skim off any foam. See
Putting Up Preserves, 50. Pour the hot
jelly into hot, sterilized jars, leaving
¼ inch headspace, 12, and process
for 5 minutes, 14.

PURE GRAPE JELLY

Prepare the recipe for *Pure
Blackberry Jelly, left*, substituting
Eastern Concord, Muscadine, or
Scuppernong grapes for the blackberries. Stem, thoroughly crush the
grapes in the pan, cook, and then
press out the juice in a colander.
Let the sediment settle as directed
in the recipe, then strain the clear
juice through a cloth to eliminate
tartrate crystals. Use 1 cup sugar
for each cup juice.

Lemon Jelly

About six ½-pint jars

This has a fine jelly consistency with the taste of marmalade. Spread it on hot breads, or serve as an unusual condiment for savory dishes.
Refer to Making Jelly, 66.
Quarter and then chop finely in a food processor:

2 pounds unpeeled lemons
8 ounces unpeeled oranges
Combine in a large, heavy saucepan with:

7½ cups water
Bring to a boil, reduce the heat, cover, and simmer 1¼ hours, stirring occasionally. Strain, 66. For each cup clear juice, add:

½ cup sugar
Cook in 2 batches. Boil rapidly, stirring frequently, to the jelling point, 48. Remove from the heat and skim off any foam. Combine the batches. See Putting Up Preserves, 50. Pour the hot jelly into hot, sterilized jars, leaving ¼-inch headspace, 12, and process for 5 minutes, 14.

ROSEMARY

From a distance, rosemary's leaves appear like diminutive pine needles on long, thin branches. The leaves are gray-green to green and sharp. Their fragrance and flavor might be described as pine mixed with mint. This is not an herb that can be subtle. Because the leaves are tough, chop them fairly fine. This releases even more of their flavor. The leaves dry well.

SAVORY LEMON JELLIES

About six ½-pint jars
Prepare the recipe for Lemon Jelly, left, blending one of the following into each jar of jelly just before sealing.

To serve with fish:
1½ teaspoons fennel seeds

To serve with chicken:
2 teaspoons finely grated ginger

To serve with beef:
½ teaspoon red pepper flakes

To serve with lamb:
Three 3½-inch sprigs rosemary

To serve with pork:
1 teaspoon cumin seeds

To serve with vegetables:
½ to 1 teaspoon ground white pepper

Apple or Crab Apple Jelly

About four ½-pint jars

This delicately flavored jelly (opposite) is invaluable for its versatility. Choose aromatic apples such as Gravenstein, Wealthy, or Cox's Orange Pippin, when available. All crab apples are excellent. Their jelly is extra rich in pectin and has a full, spicy flavor.

Refer to *Making Jelly*, 66.

Chop in ¼-inch pieces:

3 pounds unpeeled green apples or crisp crab apples

Place in a large, heavy saucepan with:

3 cups water

Cover, bring to a boil, then reduce the heat and simmer, mashing and stirring frequently, until the fruit is thoroughly soft, 20 to 25 minutes for apples, 20 to 30 minutes for crab apples. Strain, 66. Expect about 1 quart juice, adding water if necessary. For each cup clear juice, add:

1 cup sugar

Stir in:

2 tablespoons bottled lemon juice

Boil rapidly, stirring frequently, to the jelling point, 48. Remove from the heat and skim off any foam. See *Putting Up Preserves*, 50. Pour the hot jelly into hot, sterilized jars, leaving ¼-inch headspace, 12, and process for 5 minutes, 14.

GUAVA JELLY

About three ½-pint jars

Prepare the recipe for *Apple or Crab Apple Jelly, above,* substituting slightly underripe chopped guavas for the apples or crab apples. Simmer until soft, about 30 minutes. Strain twice. In place of the lemon juice, use 2 tablespoons lime juice.

QUINCE JELLY

About three ½-pint jars

Rich in pectin and delicate in flavor, quinces are excellent fruit for jelly-making.

Prepare the recipe for *Apple or Crab Apple Jelly, above,* using 3½ pounds quinces and 7 cups water. Simmer about 30 minutes.

TART PLUM JELLY

About three ½-pint jars

Plum juice is rich and needs water. Prepare the recipe for *Apple or Crab Apple Jelly, above,* using 12 ounces plums and 1⅔ to 3¼ cups water, depending on the thickness of the juice. Omit the lemon juice. Simmer for 15 to 20 minutes.

GUAVAS

The common guava—the one most available here—resembles a pale smooth-skinned lemon. Its juicy flesh is a luscious shade of pink and has an intensely sweet flowery-fruity flavor. If you live in Florida or southern California, you may also find strawberry and lemon guavas at a farmers' market. They are smaller than the common variety but have the same rich flavor. Choose blemish-free fruits, as yellow and soft as you can find, and ripen them at room temperature, out of the sun, or in a closed paper bag. Ripening time is unpredictable, so check daily and turn the fruits often.

Paradise Jelly

About seven ½-pint jars

A family favorite, this delicate jelly (above) with its exquisite rose color has been included in every JOY since the 1931 edition. Less sugar makes a darker, fruitier jelly.

Refer to *Making Jelly*, 66.

Cut into ¼-inch pieces; then place in separate large, heavy saucepans:

3 pounds unpeeled green apples
1½ pounds quinces

Add to the apples:

3 cups water

Add to the quinces:

3½ cups water

Pick over, chop coarsely, and combine in another saucepan:

½ pound cranberries
⅔ cup water

Bring to a boil, reduce the heat, and simmer until the fruit is thoroughly soft: cranberries, about 10 minutes; apples and quinces, about 25 minutes. Strain, 66. Combine the juices. Divide the juice in half and for each cup clear juice, add:

1 cup sugar

Cook in 2 batches. Boil rapidly, stirring frequently to prevent sticking, to the jelling point, 48. Remove from the heat and skim off any foam. Combine the batches. See *Putting Up Preserves*, 50. Pour the hot jelly into hot, sterilized jars, leaving ¼-inch headspace, 12, and process for 5 minutes, 14.

Pure Red or White Currant Jelly

About three ½-pint jars

This very old technique makes exquisite jelly. No water is added, and the jelly is only lightly cooked. Serve on breads, as a savory or sweet glaze, or with white meats. Do not can this jelly but refrigerate after it sets. It may keep as long as 6 months.

Refer to *Making Jelly*, 66.

Thoroughly crush in a large, heavy saucepan:

3 pounds stemmed or 3¾ pounds unstemmed red or white currants

Cover, bring to a boil, then turn the heat to low and simmer until colorless, about 10 minutes, mashing frequently. Strain, 66. For each cup juice add:

¾ cup to 1 cup sugar

Boil rapidly to the jelling point, 48. Pour into hot, sterilized jars, set on the lids and rings (see *Putting Up Preserves*, 50), and put in a warm place without disturbing until delicately set, at least 24 hours. Refrigerate.

Pomegranate Jelly

About five ½-pint jars

Everyone who receives this as a gift asks for more. Pomegranate juice extracted with an orange juicer is more bitter than juice pressed from the seeds in a food mill, but the sugar compensates for this and the jelly is not bitter.

Refer to *Making Jelly*, 66.

Extract 4 cups juice from:

3½ to 5 pounds ripe pomegranates

Strain, 66, into a glass container and refrigerate for 12 hours. Pour off the clear juice and strain again. Combine in a large, heavy saucepan:

3½ cups pomegranate juice
5 tablespoons powdered pectin (one 1.75-ounce package), 44

Stir and bring to a rolling boil over high heat. Mix in:

3½ cups sugar

Return to a rolling boil, stirring constantly, and boil according to package directions. See *Putting Up Preserves*, 50. Pour the hot jelly into hot, sterilized jars, leaving ¼-inch headspace, 12, and process for 5 minutes, 14.

POMEGRANATES

Pomegranates, with their tart-sweet ruby seeds, are in season autumn through December. Pomegranates are picked ripe. The fruits should be heavy for their size and burstingly plump. The crown should be slightly soft when gently pressed, and the leathery rind should be lustrous rather than dull and dry. When using the fruits in a centerpiece, leave them at room temperature as briefly as possible, for they dry out in warmth. However, refrigerated in a perforated plastic bag, the fruits keep for up to 2 weeks. Pomegranate seeds, tightly covered and stored in the refrigerator, will stay fresh for up to 2 days.

Mint Jelly

About four ½-pint jars

The classic accompaniment to roast lamb. Make this jelly in the summer when mint is plentiful and aromatic. The two mints we commonly use for cooking are peppermint and spearmint.
Refer to *Making Jelly*, 66.
Place in a large, heavy saucepan and thoroughly crush:

1½ cups packed fresh mint leaves
Add:

1½ cups apple juice

½ cup bottled lemon juice
Bring to a boil over high heat. Remove from the heat, cover, and let stand for 10 minutes. Strain, 66. Expect about 1¾ cups of juice, adding water if necessary. Return the mint juice to the saucepan, adding:

3½ cups sugar
4 drops green food coloring (optional)
¾ teaspoon salt

Bring to a boil, stirring constantly. Add:

3 ounces liquid pectin, 44
Boil hard for 1 minute. Remove from the heat and skim off any foam. See *Putting Up Preserves*, 50. Pour the hot jelly into hot, sterilized jars, leaving ¼-inch headspace, 12, and process for 5 minutes, 14.

Prickly Pear Jelly

About five ½-pint jars

Refer to *Making Jelly*, 66.
Slice in half and, with the tip of a spoon, scrape the pulp into a large, heavy saucepan from:

4½ pounds ripe prickly pears, below, halved
Mash thoroughly, then blend in:

1 cup water
Bring to a boil, stirring frequently, then remove from the heat. Strain, 66.

You'll need 3 cups juice. If there is more, simmer it down to 3 cups. Pour the juice into a large, heavy saucepan and add:

6 tablespoons strained lime juice
2 tablespoons strained orange juice
5 tablespoons powdered pectin (one 1.75-ounce package), 44
Stir and bring to a rolling boil over high heat. Mix in:

4 cups sugar
Stirring constantly, return to a rolling boil, and boil according to package directions. See *Putting Up Preserves*, 50. Pour the hot jelly into hot, sterilized jars, leaving ¼-inch headspace, 12, and process for 5 minutes, 14.

PRICKLY PEARS

In this country, these juicy berries the size and shape of an egg are most often purplish red or deep yellow. In others parts of the world, they may be cream colored, chartreuse, pink, or even purple verging on black. They have many names: cactus or Indian or Barbary pear or Indian fig, *tuna* (Spanish), or *sabra* (Hebrew). The fruits are prickly outside but watermelon sweet inside. Prickly pears are filled with small seeds, and in some varieties, the seeds are edible. Most fruits are harvested in the West from August through December. The fruits grow with small rosettes of spines scattered over their peel. Select ripe fruits, but to test them, pick each one up with a folded paper bag, since there may be bits of needles still in their flesh. The spines are supposed to be removed before the fruit is shipped, but there is no guarantee. Those prickly pears that yield when gently pressed between your hands are ready. Store at cool room temperature. When they are ripe, refrigerate in a perforated plastic bag for up to 2 days

Hot Pepper Jelly

About three ½-pint jars

The balance of hot and sweet flavors is delicious with corn bread (above), or as a glaze for sautéed chicken and pork. Ripe red peppers give the jelly a translucent orange-red appearance.

Refer to *Making Jelly*, 66.

Mince or grind:

1 pound ripe sweet red peppers, cored and seeded

8 ounces jalapeño peppers (remove seeds to make them less hot)

Combine the peppers and their juices in a large, heavy saucepan with:

1½ cups white wine vinegar

Stir and bring to simmer over medium heat until the peppers are thoroughly soft, 10 to 12 minutes. Strain, 66. Expect about 2 cups of juice, adding water if necessary. Return the pepper juice to the saucepan, adding:

2½ cups sugar

Bring to a boil, stirring constantly. Add:

3 ounces liquid pectin, 44

Boil hard for 1 minute. Remove from the heat and skim off any foam. See *Putting Up Preserves*, 50. Pour the hot jelly into hot, sterilized jars, leaving ¼-inch headspace, 12, and process for 5 minutes, 14.

Making and Cooking Marmalade

Marmalade is best described as a jelly with small pieces of fruit—most often citrus peel, but other firm fruits work well. Like jam, there is leeway in marmalade—it can be soft or firm—but like jelly, the juice should be clear and the pectin and acid contents high. Because the syrup of citrus marmalade jells, cooking is the same as for jelly.

Please read the directions for safe and proper canning, 8 to 19, before proceeding. Pour hot marmalades into hot, sterilized jars, leaving ¼-inch headspace, 12, and process in a boiling-water canner for 10 minutes, 14.

Preparing Citrus Fruits

Choose citrus that is heavy for its size—it will be the juiciest. The color of the rind has no bearing on the interior quality. When blood oranges are available, their garnet color makes gorgeous marmalade. As other uncommon citrus come along—limequats, pomelos, ugli fruit—try them in place of bitter oranges in the recipe for *Bitter Orange Marmalade* that follows.

Chilling citrus makes it easier to slice very thinly. Use a stainless-steel knife (carbon steel reacts with acid and stains the fruit). The center of a citrus fruit is tough; remove it for better marmalade. Begin by slicing fruits in half, then use scissors to snip around the white area just outside where the points of the segments meet (**1**). Snip all the way down, then lift out the centers, and flick out the seeds. Since seeds and centers are rich in pectin, tie them in a single layer of cheesecloth (**2**) and add the bag to the fruit. At the end of the cooking, squeeze the juice from the bag and blend it into the marmalade.

The spongy white pith just under the citrus peel is where most of the pectin lies, so always include some in marmalade. End slices that are pure peel and pith are best cut into strips (**3**) the thickness of the other pieces. Tenderizing citrus peel is crucial to marmalade. Soak the prepared fruit and peel in water in a cool place overnight. The next day, cover and simmer until the peel is thoroughly tender. This takes from 15 minutes to more than an hour, depending on the size and thickness of the fruit slices. To test, cut a piece against the side of the pan with the edge of a wooden spoon—it should instantly fall in half if done (**4**).

Bitter Orange Marmalade

About ten ½-pint jars

In winter, look for bitter Seville oranges or blood oranges or make sweet orange marmalade with 1½ pounds sweet oranges and 1 pound lemons. For amber marmalade, use half brown sugar.

Chill, then halve crosswise, snip out tough centers, and thinly slice, removing any seeds:

2 pounds unpeeled bitter oranges

8 ounces unpeeled lemons

Combine in a bowl with their juice and add:

8 cups water

Cover and let stand overnight in the refrigerator, then simmer until the citrus peel is tender. Divide in half the mixture and:

6½ cups sugar

Cook in 2 batches. Boil rapidly, stirring frequently, to the jelling point, 48. Remove from the heat and skim off any foam. Combine the batches before packing into hot jars. See *Putting Up Preserves*, 50. Leave ¼-inch headspace, 12, and process for 10 minutes, 14.

BITTER OR SOUR ORANGES

Bitter oranges, often called sour oranges, are not grown on a wide scale commercially, but in late winter and early spring they can be found in Latin-American markets and farmers' markets in citrus-growing country. These oranges—Seville, Bouquet de Fleurs, and Chinotto—are marmalade oranges. While acidic, they have a bitter aftertaste that is the hallmark of orange marmalade.

Kiwi and Meyer Lemon Marmalade

About eight ½-pint jars

If you cannot find Meyer lemons, use a mix of lemon and sweet oranges for these delicate preserves.
Chill, then halve crosswise, snip out tough centers, and thinly slice, removing any seeds:

1¼ pounds unpeeled Meyer lemons (or 1 pound any lemons and 4 ounces sweet oranges)

Combine in a bowl with:

4 cups water

Cover and let stand overnight in the refrigerator, then simmer until the peel is tender, about 15 minutes.

Peel, slice ¼ inch thick, and gently stir into the citrus:

1½ pounds firm-ripe kiwi

Divide in half the fruit and:

5 cups sugar

Cook in 2 batches. Boil rapidly, stirring carefully to keep the kiwi slices as intact as possible, to the jelling point, 48. Remove from the heat and skim off any foam. Combine the batches before packing into hot jars. See *Putting Up Preserves*, 50. Leave ¼-inch headspace, 12, and process for 10 minutes, 14.

MEYER LEMONS

Meyer lemons, first imported to America from China in 1980, are a cross between lemon and mandarin. Their rind is bright yellow and very thin. Their juicy flesh is warm gold with a tangy sweet flavor hinting of citrus blossoms. Meyer lemons ripen all year, but your best chance of finding them is in specialty markets winter through spring.

Ginger Marmalade

About four ½-pint jars

Spread these invigorating preserves on English muffins or rich meats, or stir into marinades and sauces. Select ginger that is not stringy. Adding the sugar in 2 stages helps plump the ginger.
Peel, thinly slice, then finely chop:

2 pounds fresh ginger

Combine in a large, heavy saucepan with:

12 cups water

Bring to a boil, reduce the heat, and simmer, stirring occasionally, until the ginger is softened, about 2 hours. Stir in:

1¼ cups apple cider
5 tablespoons bottled lemon juice
5 tablespoons light corn syrup
Measure:

4 cups sugar

Stir 3 cups of the sugar into the ginger mixture and boil gently for 15 minutes. Set in a cool place overnight. Bring to a simmer, add the remaining 1 cup sugar, and simmer, stirring often, until the spoon cuts a path through the marmalade, 45 minutes to 1 hour. Pack the hot marmalade into hot jars. See *Putting Up Preserves*, 50. Leave ¼-inch headspace, 12, and process for 10 minutes, 14.

Four Citrus Marmalade

About eight ½-pint jars

Cut off the peel and ⅛-inch pith from:

1½ pounds grapefruit, preferably ruby
1 pound sweet oranges
8 ounces tender-skinned limes, Bearss if possible, below
8 ounces lemons

Chop the peel into ¼-inch pieces by hand, or in a food processor with:

2 cups water

Combine the peel and water in a saucepan and simmer until the peel is soft, 5 to 10 minutes. Cut off and discard the remaining white pith from the fruits. Cut the fruits in half and remove the centers and seeds. Chop the pulp into ¼-inch pieces. Mix the peel and pulp in a bowl with:

4 cups water

Cover and let stand overnight in the refrigerator. Divide in half the mixture and:

5½ cups sugar

Cook in 2 batches. Boil rapidly, stirring frequently, to the jelling point, 48. Remove from the heat and skim off any foam. Combine the batches before packing into hot jars. See *Putting Up Preserves*, 50. Leave ¼-inch headspace, 12, and process for 10 minutes, 14.

LIMES

There are two if not three types of true limes. One group, called the Bartender's lime, is made up of Mexican limes, Key limes, and West Indian limes. They are small and oval. Commercially, they are picked green when they are at their most sour. When they turn yellow-orange, they are mature. Their pulp is pale with a splendidly tart, aromatic flavor. Seedless Bearss limes are larger, the size of a small lemon. For the most flavor select Bearss when green—ripe, they are greenish yellow inside and out. Their flavor is bright but less intense than that of the Mexican lime group. Some believe Bearss is a separate type, and some regard it as a variety of Persian or Tahitian lime because it is almost identical. Some form of true lime is available year round. Select firm, glossy, heavy fruits.

Making Fruit Butter

Fruit butters—fruit purees cooked slowly until thick—earn their name for their smooth, spreadable consistency. Fruit butters are thickened by the evaporation of water, resulting in deeply concentrated fruit flavors. Born of thrift, fruit butters contain the least sugar of all preserves and are often accented with spices (**1**).

The challenge in making fruit butters is to cook them slowly for several hours without scorching. For the best flavor, begin by cooking the whole fruit, much like jelly. Put it through a food mill (**2**) to remove the inedible parts and slowly simmer the strained pulp until it becomes thick enough to mound on a spoon (**3**). Fruits can be oven cooked in both stages.

Please read the directions for safe and proper canning, 8 to 19, before proceeding. Pack hot fruit butters into hot half-pint or pint jars, leaving ¼-inch headspace, 12, and process in a boiling-water canner for 10 minutes, 14, unless otherwise noted.

Baked Apple Butter

About eight ½-pint jars

This is the easiest, and perhaps finest, apple butter of all.
Stem and quarter:

6 pounds unpeeled cooking apples, such as Cortland and Macoun

Combine in a large, heavy saucepan with:

8 cups apple juice or water

Cover and simmer, stirring occasionally, until the apples are soft, about 1½ hours. Preheat the oven to 200°F. Pass the apples through a food mill or medium-mesh sieve. Return to the pan, and add:

Juice and grated zest of 1 lemon

1¼ cups sugar (half may be brown sugar)

1½ teaspoons ground cinnamon
¾ teaspoon ground cloves
¼ teaspoon ground allspice

Slowly bring to a boil, stirring frequently. Stir in:

½ cup port or dry red wine (optional)

Pour three-quarters of the puree into a crock or deep baking dish, reserving the rest. Bake, uncovered, until thick enough to mound on a spoon, about 10 hours. As the mixture shrinks, add the reserved puree. Pack the hot fruit butter into hot jars. See *Putting Up Preserves*, 50. Leave ¼-inch headspace, 12, and process for 10 minutes, 14.

> **NATURALLY SWEETENED APPLE BUTTER**
>
> *Try Gala, Golden Delicious, Northern Spy, or Wealthy for this pure apple variation.*
> Prepare the recipe for *Baked Apple Butter, left,* using sweet cooking apples and omitting the sugar. Replace the wine with thawed frozen unsweetened apple juice concentrate. When the puree is thick, stir in a pinch of salt and sweetener to taste. Leave ¼-inch headspace, 12, and process for 15 minutes, 14.

Microwave Honey Butter

About four ½-pint jars

Microwave-cooked fruit butter is lighter in color and flavor than baked.
Finely puree the pulp left in the jelly bag after making jelly, 68. Mix together thoroughly in a microwave-safe container:

3¾ cups pureed fruit pulp
¾ cup mild honey

1 tablespoon bottled lemon juice
2¾ teaspoons ground cinnamon
¾ teaspoon ground mace or nutmeg

Cover with waxed paper, place in the microwave, and cook on high until nearly thick enough to mound up on a spoon. Stir every 5 minutes. If desired, add:

About 1 tablespoon brandy (optional)

Pack the hot fruit butter into hot jars. See *Putting Up Preserves*, 50. Leave ¼-inch headspace, 12, and process for 10 minutes, 14.

Making Jellied Fruit Sauces

Jellied fruit sauces are made from thick fruit puree, like fruit butter, but they rely on pectin for their luscious firm texture. These dense preserves, also called fruit cheese, are aged for 6 to 24 months and then unmolded and sliced—much like the familiar canned jellied cranberry sauce. The flavor is incomparable.

It's best to age jellied fruit for at least 6 months before serving—their flavor develops for up to 2 years, and the preserves keep at their best for up to 3 years. To serve, run a table knife around the inside of the jar, being careful not to damage the glass, shake out the preserves, and slice ½ inch thick. Studded with chopped almonds and surrounded with port or cream, they make a superb dessert.

Please read the directions for safe and proper canning, 8 to 19, before proceeding. The trick to the preserves is boiling the puree rapidly to develop the pectin. When boiling, the puree erupts, so wear an apron, long sleeves, and protective glasses. Stir constantly with a long-handled spoon, scraping around the edges of the pan and thoroughly across every inch of the bottom. The preserves are ready when you can see the bottom of the pan when you pull a spoon through the center of the puree. Lightly oil the insides of sterilized widemouthed straight-sided pint jars with a neutral-tasting vegetable oil to help the jellied fruit slide out of the jars. Fill the pint jars leaving ½-inch headspace, 12, and process in a boiling-water canner for 15 minutes (the longer processing time is needed to penetrate these dense preserves), 14.

Jellied Damson Sauce

About five 1-pint jars

For a quick and excellent dessert, top with chopped almonds and a dollop of whipped cream, opposite.
Preheat the oven to 275°F. Brush the insides of sterilized widemouthed straight-sided pint jars with:

Vegetable oil
Stem, then place in a 4½-quart crock or earthenware bowl, or in 2 large bowls:

6 pounds Damson plums
Cover and bake until simmering and syrupy, about 2½ hours. Push the hot pulp through a food mill or a colander with a pestle or wooden spoon, discarding the pits. Divide in half the puree and:

8 cups sugar
Cook in 2 batches. Bring the puree to a simmer in a broad, heavy 7- to 8-quart saucepan over low heat. Add the sugar. When the sugar dissolves, boil over high heat, stirring, until you can see the bottom of the pan when you pull a spoon through the center of the puree, about 9 to 10 minutes. Pour the hot preserves into the prepared jars. If desired, press into the top of the jars before sealing:

1 fresh bay leaf (optional)
See *Putting Up Preserves*, 50. Leave ½-inch headspace, 12, and process for 15 minutes, 14.

MORE JELLIED SAUCES

The method used for *Jellied Damson Sauce, above*, also works well with other tart plums, as well as with tart green apples, barely ripe quinces, cranberries, and tart blackberries. Use 1½ cups sugar per pound of puree.

Preserving Fruits in Spirits

Spirits (alcoholic beverages) preserve food the way vinegar does, by eliminating potential contaminants. Fruits preserved in spirits can be spooned over ice cream or used in puddings and compotes. The syrup is strained into a bottle and used to flavor fruits and desserts and, of course, sipped in cordial glasses. Brandy or *eau-de-vie* (a form of brandy) is traditional abroad, but in this country, bourbon is often used instead with great success.

Here we offer recipes for apricots, peaches, and cherries. Also try small whole plums and peeled, small whole pears. In all cases, the fruits darken, but this does not mean that the process has gone wrong. The fruits will hold their flavor for a year or so; the spirits will virtually keep forever. Jars for these mixtures do not need to be sterilized because of the alcohol content. However, a cool storage (less than 45°F) is essential.

Brandied Cherries

1 pound fruit makes one 1-pint jar

This old French recipe is the easiest method of preserving summer fruits.
Snip the stems down to ½ inch, then weigh:
Plump ripe sweet cherries
For every 1 pound of fruit, measure:
Heaping ½ cup sugar
Layer the fruit and sugar in pint jars. Fill the jars to ¼ inch from the top with:
Brandy, kirsch, framboise, marc, grappa, vodka, or bourbon
Cap tightly and wrap in brown paper. Let stand in a cool, dark, dry place for 7 to 8 weeks before serving. For the first month or so, occasionally rock the jars back and forth to help the sugar melt and to distribute the flavors.

Brandied Peaches

1 pound fruit makes one 1-pint jar

Blanch and remove the skins from:
Small firm-ripe peaches
Pack the peaches into 1-pint jars. Cover them completely with:
Sugar
Shake the jars to make sure the sugar fills all the spaces. Cover the jars loosely. Set in a cool, dark place where you can keep an eye on them. As the sugar dissolves, continue to cover the peaches with more sugar. When syrup covers the fruit, fill the jars to ¼ inch from the top with:
Brandy or bourbon
Cap tightly, wrap the jars in brown paper or cloth, and place in a cool, dark, dry place. The peaches may be ready to serve in 3 months, or they may take longer.

Brandied Apricots

1 pound fruit makes one 1-pint jar

These fruits have a mild brandy flavor because the brandy is diluted with water. As a result, potential contaminants must be destroyed before putting the jars away. Lightly cook the fruit, then process the filled jars in a boiling-water bath, 14. If you prefer a stronger spirit flavor, use 1½ cups sugar for every 1 cup water. After poaching the fruit, boil down the syrup until the consistency of maple syrup, then cover the fruit with equal parts syrup and brandy.

Weigh, blanch, and remove the skins from:

Firm-ripe apricots or other fruits, all the same size

Prepare a syrup in a large, heavy saucepan, combining for every 1 pound fruit:

1 cup sugar

1 cup water

Stir until the sugar is dissolved. Bring the syrup to a boil and add the fruit. Simmer until the fruit is barely tender when tested with a thin skewer, about 5 minutes. Pack into hot, sterilized jars, fitting the fruit tightly without crushing. Pour the simmering syrup over the fruit, filling the jars three-quarters full. Add to the top, leaving ¼-inch headspace, 12:

Brandy, kirsch, framboise, vodka, or bourbon

Process for 10 minutes, 14. Let stand in a cool, dark, dry place for at least 1 month before serving.

ABOUT
PICKLING &
SALTING

*P*ickling is the art of preserving food in acid. Acid is either added to the food, or the food itself produces acid through fermentation.

Salting has been used for thousands of years as a method of preserving food. Often used in conjunction with pickling, salting also turns cabbage into sauerkraut and cures olives.

From left: Quick Dill Pickles, 101, and Salt-Cured Black Olives, 109

Pickling Methods

There are two basic methods of introducing acid to food, or pickling. In the **direct method**—called quick pickling or short brining—food is covered in vinegar, and that is that. Foods most commonly quick-pickled are fruits and vegetables. Vinegars used for quick pickling are apple cider vinegar and white vinegar, both containing 5 percent pure acetic acid. The flavor of quick pickles is fresh and sharp, but will mellow after a few weeks. Fruit and sweet vegetable pickles have sugar mixed with their acid for a sweet-tangy taste.

In the **indirect method**—often called salting, long brining, fermentation, or curing—vinegar is not required, because the food creates its own acid. Pickling begins by either salting directly or by brining (brine is salt in liquid, normally water, and usually in high concentration). Just enough salt is used to keep harmful microorganisms at bay while allowing the bacteria that cause fermentation to multiply. Fermentation produces lactic acid, the ultimate preserver, and can take weeks, even months. Slowly developed, the flavors of these pickled foods are deep and rich. Crock-cured pickles and sauerkraut are prepared this way.

Many variations on the two basic methods have emerged. For vegetables, it is popular to combine salting and vinegaring. Vegetables are soaked in brine from 3 to 24 hours. This draws out moisture, which firms the vegetable and helps make it crisp. The vegetable is then drained from the brine and combined with vinegar, which penetrates the food and preserves it.

SAFE PICKLING

Many old-fashioned recipes have been dropped from responsible pickling books because the recipes do not conform to modern safety guidelines. Although putting up pickles is simple, the pickling process is extraordinarily complex, and potential harm can come from improvising.

Clostridium botulinum is a dangerous bacterium that flourishes in moist, airless, low-acid, room-temperature environments. It seems impossible that a pickled food can be low-acid, but it can happen if a low-acid food has not been permeated by vinegar. To be safe, only use tested up-to-date pickling recipes, such as those in this chapter, and follow them to the letter.

Acids

Acid inhibits the growth of destructive microorganisms. Pickled vegetables and fruits retain a fresh texture and appearance.

VINEGARS

For safety's sake, it is essential to use a high-grade vinegar with a content of at least 5 percent acetic acid (sometimes labeled 50 grain). Cider vinegar and distilled white vinegar are both recommended. Cider vinegar is preferred for its mellow fruity flavor, but its color darkens the pickle over time. Distilled white vinegar is clear and ideal for most quick pickling, but it is sharp. Occasionally, for smoothness, we blend the two vinegars or add bottled lemon juice, which is dependably high in acid. If a recipe's vinegar solution seems strong for your taste, remember it will mellow with curing. **Never reduce the proportion of vinegar called for in a recipe.**

Balsamic and malt vinegars may contain 6 percent acetic acid and are both effective in pickling. However, because their flavors may overwhelm the flavor of the food being pickled, it is best to mix them with cider or white vinegar. Most vinegars made from wine, fruit, and rice have 4.3 percent acetic acid and are not strong enough. If the label does not give the vinegar's acid content, do not use it for pickling. Do not use homemade vinegars because their acid content is unknown.

From left: Pickled Red Onion Rings, 98, and Dilly Beans, 98

Salt and Sugar

Salt is the primary preservative and flavor enhancer in brining. We recommend using **pickling salt** or **canning salt,** which do not contain additives that can cloud the vinegar solution. Do not use flaked salt, which varies in density, or iodized salt, which can darken pickles. For fermented pickles, do not use light salts. For dry curing, coarse-grained kosher salt or coarse sea salt is occasionally used.

Sugar flavors food, intensifies color, and helps plump and firm fruits and vegetables. It also nourishes beneficial bacteria produced while food is curing. Brown sugar lends caramel color and flavor. Artificial sweeteners can be used as well, but they do not actually contribute to the preserving process. Follow the manufacturer's directions for substituting for sugar.

Water

Soft water is preferable for pickling; minerals in hard water can interfere with the formation of acid and the curing process. Heavily chlorinated water cannot make a sweet brine.

If soft tap water is unavailable, either use distilled water or boil the water for 15 minutes, cover, and let stand for 24 hours. Skim off any scum on top, then carefully pour off the clear water, leaving the sediment behind. Add 1 tablespoon 5 percent acetic-acid vinegar to each gallon before using.

Crisping Agents

In old-fashioned recipes, alum and pickling lime were sometimes added to ensure crisp pickles. The calcium in pickling lime (also known as slaked lime or calcium hydroxide) does make pickles firm, but it can make the pickles bitter, and rinsing several times is a nuisance. Too much alum can be unsafe and is no longer recommended. When today's techniques and fresh prime ingredients are used, pickles can be crisp without chemicals.

Our favorite crisping technique is to place a 2- to 3-inch layer of crushed or cubed ice over vegetables while they are brining. This aids crispness and helps keep pieces from breaking when they are heated. A wet towel between the ice and the foods lets the cold through but eliminates having to pick ice out of the food at the end. Add more ice as needed.

Fine crisping agents also grow in the wild: leaves of grape vines (especially Scuppernong), cherry trees, black currant bushes, and oak trees contain a substance that blocks enzymes from softening vegetables—cucumbers, particularly. Thoroughly wash unsprayed leaves and layer them with cucumbers during brining, then discard the leaves.

Herbs and Spices

Fresh leaves of herbs and whole dried spices hold up best in pickles. Ground spices will cloud the vinegar solution, although sometimes it is worth sacrificing clarity for intensity of flavor. Bay leaves are especially potent—simmer one or two in the vinegar solution, then remove before canning. Mustard seed is a common spice used in pickling, adding both flavor and texture. Yellow, brown, and black mustard seeds are interchangeable in these recipes. Ground turmeric is a favorite pickler's spice because a very little brightens color. For example, corn relish before the turmeric is pale—after the turmeric, it glows. **Mixed pickling spice** is readily purchased in grocery stores and is generally a ground blend of mustard seeds, cinnamon, ginger, bay leaves, pepper, allspice, caraway seeds, cloves, mace, and cardamom.

Produce

Select the freshest available fruits and vegetables, perfectly ripe for eating, without a trace of mold or blemishes. The importance of freshness cannot be emphasized strongly enough. If pickling cannot be started within 24 hours of harvest, refrigerate the food and use as soon as possible. Many fruits and vegetables are un predictable in terms of size, weight, and yield. One pound of Seckel pears may fill a quart jar, a pint jar, or even less. Prepare to be flexible.

CUCUMBERS

Especially when pickled whole, the short, blocky varieties of cucumbers bred specifically for pickling give superior results. Their tissues absorb brine and sustain processing without softening. For bread-and-butter pickles, long, cylindrical slicing cucumbers can be used in a pinch, but not the very long cucumbers such as Asian burpless or English hothouse. These may contain an enzyme that can cause the pickles to soften.

Standard pickle length is 4 inches. For tiny gherkins and cornichons, choose varieties bred to be harvested around 1½ inches long, although some pickling cucumbers are successful when harvested small. Small, rounded West Indian gherkins absorb brine and syrup like sponges and make prize pickles. Misshapen cucumbers or those that float when washed (being hollow) can be used in relishes.

Equipment

Do not use utensils made of materials that react with acid—that includes aluminum, brass, copper, galvanized or zinc-coated metal and cast iron. For simmering food, use stainless steel, unchipped enamel, or unchipped graniteware. A large, deep, heavy skillet—roughly 11¾ inches by 2¼ inches deep—accommodates most ingredients in these recipes for simmering in a single layer. For crock curing—steeping food in acidic ingredients—crocks, jars, pots, bowls, and buckets of uncracked stoneware, unchipped enamel, glass, stainless steel, and food-grade plastic are the only containers safe to use. Allow 1 gallon in size for every 5 pounds of food. This allows several inches of essential air space between the food and the top of the container.

In addition to making slices more interesting, a crinkle-edged cutter (above) leaves more surface area exposed to the vinegar solution. Crinkle-edged cutters are available at cookware stores.

Preparation

It's best to have your equipment and preparation area cleaned and ready and your nonperishable ingredients set out before you begin preparing the fruits or vegetables. Wash crocks in very hot soapy water, rinse, and dry thoroughly. An effective disinfectant for washing cutting boards and utensils is one part chlorine bleach to nine parts water. Rinse thoroughly with water before using.

When washing fruits and vegetables, scrub particularly around stems, blossom ends, and crevices—these are hiding places for bacteria. Most bacteria grow best on low-acid foods—which means almost everything but fruit. Taking into consideration the temperatures and speed at which bacteria grow, food scientists have given us the two-hour rule: Raw foods susceptible to bacterial contaminiation should not be left between 40° and 140°F for more than two hours.

Specific instructions are in each recipe; however, keep in mind that the blossom end of cucumbers contains an enzyme that may soften pickles, so slice ¹⁄₁₆ inch off that end (if you are not sure which end that is, trim both ends). Also, when pickling chili peppers whole, slash through once or twice with a thin knife, so the vinegar solution can seep inside.

For uniformity of pickling and processing, sort pieces so all in the container are of similar size. If the goal is the crispest possible texture, ½ inch should be the maximum thickness of slices for thick, crisp vegetables, and 1 inch is the maximum for thickness for softer vegetables and fruits.

SIMMERING THE FOOD

Place the prepared food without crowding in a nonreactive, large, deep, heavy pan on a burner. Cover with the simmering liquid, turn the heat to high, and set the timer when the liquid returns to a boil. Maintain a simmer or gentle boil and stir frequently. As in canning, the cooking liquid of vegetables that harbor an uncommon amount of potential spoilage—root vegetables, for example—is always discarded. Follow the directions given in the recipes.

TEMPERATURES

Fruits and vegetables may not ferment at all below 60°F. For the unrefrigerated brining of vegetables, 60° to 65°F will produce the highest quality, and fermentation will take between 4 and 6 weeks. For safety's sake, food must be completely covered with either vinegar solution or brine. For quick-pickling vegetables at room temperature—70° to 75°F—it will take 3 to 4 weeks. The pickle will be good, but not as good as at the lower temperature. Above 80°F, the pickle will be too soft or may spoil. **Caution:** If, in the process of fermenting, the food becomes soft or slimy, or develops a disagreeable odor, discard it without tasting according to the directions on 97.

directions on 97.

USING YOUR TIME WISELY

If you choose recipes using a variety of techniques—easily found in this section—you can have a few bowls chilling in the refrigerator, a crock or two fermenting in a corner, some foods ready for simmering, and some ready to pack for processing—all while jars are sterilizing on a back burner. Fresh unused vinegar solution may be covered and refrigerated for a week or two—doubling or tripling the recipe can save time. Vinegar solution that has been used for simmering can be covered and refrigerated and added to marinades, salad dressings, and sauces within 1 to 2 days.

Putting Up Pickles

There are two ways of keeping your homemade pickles—refrigeration and canning.

REFRIGERATION

You can refrigerate any quick pickle without processing the jar in a boiling-water bath, but the jar should still be sterilized. Unprocessed pickles and opened processed pickles will keep from 2 to 4 weeks in the refrigerator, perhaps longer. Few pickles freeze well.

Many salted foods keep without canning if stored in a cool, dry place or in the refrigerator.

CANNING

Please read the directions for safe and proper canning, 8 to 19, before proceeding. Unless pickles are to be stored in the refrigerator, processing is essential for safety. The heat of processing also inactivates enzymes that would affect the flavor, color, and texture of the pickles, and the seal keeps new contaminants out. Being a high-acid food, pickles are not pressure-canned but are processed in a boiling-water bath. Pickles processed for less than 10 minutes must go into sterilized jars (see *Equipment*, 11). Unless otherwise noted, pack hot pickles and liquid into hot jars (see *Packing Jars*, 12) leaving a ½-inch headspace, 12. Wipe the rims clean, and set on the lids. Screw the rings on firmly. Process for the appropriate time given in the recipe, following instructions under *Boiling-Water Canning*, 14, then *Cooling the Jars*, 16, and *Storing Canned Goods*, 17. Pickling recipes can be halved or doubled, but the processing time for each jar remains the same.

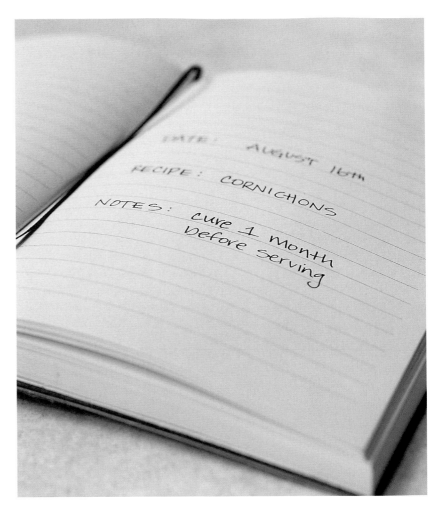

A pint jar (preferably wide-mouthed) is ideal for pickles, because the vinegar solution and the heat in processing can evenly reach each piece. A pint jar holds 2 cups pickles plus ¾ to 1 cup vinegar solution. As with canning, do not alter or experiment with processing times and jar sizes. Also, if a jar is only partially filled, do not process. Instead, refrigerate and eat the contents within 2 to 4 weeks. Unopened processed pickles will keep in a cool, dark, dry place for at least 1 year.

Wrap jars of bright-colored pickles in heavy brown paper.

With time, some pickles grow crisper and more subtle, some grow softer and stronger. It is a good idea to keep track with a notebook. Always include the date and batch number if applicable, as well as the variety of vegetable or fruit, when you can. Note on your calendar when a step in the pickling process is due—check the crock for scum, turn the food, remove the food from the brine, and so on.

Troubleshooting

We learn by our mistakes. The following are valuable lessons.

When pickled food has an unpleasantly bitter or strong taste, the vinegar may have been old. Another possibility is that potassium chloride was used; this salt substitute is naturally bitter and is not generally recommended for pickling. Incompatible spices, or spices simmered too long, or too many spices in the mixture, could also make the mixture bitter. Finally, unpeeled vegetables or fruits can have disappointing results, as many peels are bitter.

Darkened or discolored pickles may be due to using iodized salt, hard water, or too many ground or dark spices. Or the pickle may have come in contact with a metal that reacted with the acid, 94. If brass, copper, or zinc utensils or equipment were used in the pickling, do not eat the pickles. If the vinegar solution has turned pink and there is overripe dill in the jar and no sign of spoilage, below, the dill caused the color change and the pickles are safe to eat. However, if there is scum or bubbling, or anything odd about the pickles, this indicates yeast growth, another cause of pink liquid, and the pickles should be discarded without tasting. Green or bluish green garlic cloves are due to a reaction with metals in the water and the pickles are safe to eat. Scum on the brine of fermenting pickles is the product of wild yeasts, molds, and bacteria. As long as the scum is removed as soon as it forms, the pickles will be fine. White sediment at the bottom of the crock during fermentation is caused by non-harmful bacteria and is not a problem.

Hollow centers can mean the cucumbers were too large to efficiently absorb the brine. If they were the right size, perhaps they were not completely covered in brine, or the brine was not strong enough. Cucumbers may become hollow if not brined within 24 hours of pickling—or perhaps the cucumber just grew that way.

Shriveled pickles may be the result of too much salt in the brine. Or the vinegar was too acidic, the syrup was too heavy, or the cooking or processing time was too long. Double-check the recipe. Cucumbers much more than 24 hours off the vine are very apt to shrivel. Spotted or faded pickles can happen if the cucumbers were not thoroughly brined (too little salt or too little time), or their jars were exposed to too much light in storing. A cucumber pickle may also soften if its blossom end—and the destructive enzyme with it—is not removed. Or it may have been a slicing instead of a pickling cucumber. As long as there are no signs of spoilage, below, pickles that have become soft are safe to eat.

Spoilage

Discard, without tasting, jars of pickles that have broken seals, surface mold, bubbles rising, or seepage or spurting liquid, or contain a disagreeable odor, are soft, slippery or slimy, emit a hiss when the lid is turned, or display any other unusual element (except those above noted as safe). The final and best advice is always, **when in doubt, throw it out!** See *Handling Contaminated Food and Jars, 19,* for directions on disposal.

HIGH-ALTITUDE PICKLING

Pickling and canning recipes have been formulated for sea level. At higher altitudes, the temperature of boiling water is lower, which means that processing times must be increased in order to can foods safely.

Increased processing times:
1,001–6,000 feet, add 5 minutes
6,001 + feet, add 10 minutes

The following exceptions have different high-altitude processing times indicated below:

Pickled Red or Golden Beets, 99
Cranberry-Pickled Pears, 104
Pickled Peaches, 104
Pickled Lemon-Melon Rind, 107

1,001–3,000 feet, add 5 minutes
3,001–6,000 feet, add 10 minutes
6,001 + feet, add 15 minutes

Dilly Beans

About one 1-pint jar

Dill is traditional in this classic recipe, but you can substitute other herbs that complement beans—mint, marjoram, tarragon, or thyme, for example. Use beans that are ⅜ inch thick or less.

Wash, trim the ends, and string if necessary:

8 ounces fresh plump snap beans, preferably round pods

The pieces should be no more than 4 inches long. Place in the hot, sterilized pint jar:

3 to 6 sprigs fresh dill or 2½ tablespoons dill seeds
1 clove garlic, peeled (optional)

1 teaspoon red pepper flakes or ¼ teaspoon ground red pepper (optional)

Closely pack the beans upright in the jar. Combine in a saucepan and bring to a boil:

½ cup white vinegar
½ cup water
1 tablespoon salt

Pour the hot vinegar solution into the jar. See *Putting Up Pickles*, 96. Leave ½-inch headspace, 12, and process for 5 minutes, 14.

SNAP BEANS

The bean pod, from a day to a week old, is tender enough to snap when folded in half. Pods can be rounded and skinny, like French filet beans or haricots verts; broad, flat, and thick, like Italian Romanos; or round, slender, and long as your arm, like Asian yard-long beans. America's great Blue Lakes and Kentucky Wonders have been developed for eating as pods. Snap beans come in green, purple, yellow, and assorted colors in between.

PICKLED ASPARAGUS

Asparagus for pickling should be very fresh with tightly closed tips.
Prepare *Dilly Beans, above,* substituting the tip ends of asparagus with tightly closed spears for the beans. Pack tips down. Process pints for 10 minutes, 14.

PICKLED OKRA

Select young, tender okra pods; the fresher, the better. Wash well and trim the cut ends only without cutting into the pods.
Prepare *Dilly Beans, above,* substituting a scant 1 pound okra for the beans. Process pints for 10 minutes, 14.

PICKLED GREEN TOMATOES

Prepare *Dilly Beans, above,* substituting a generous 12 ounces small green tomatoes for the beans. Wash, stem, core, and halve or quarter the tomatoes (to be ⅜ inch thick). Add a small bay leaf to the jar, if desired. Process pints for 15 minutes, 14.

Pickled Red Onion Rings

About six ½-pint jars

These rings make a crunchy addition to scrambled eggs, sandwiches, sauces, and sautés.

Wash, peel, and cut into ¼-inch-thick slices:

2 pounds red onions up to 2½ inches wide

Separate the slices into rings. Tie in a cloth:

1 large bay leaf
2 large cloves garlic, peeled and crushed through a garlic press

Combine in a large, deep skillet and bring to a boil, stirring until the sugar is dissolved:

2⅔ cups cider vinegar
¼ cup bottled lemon juice
⅓ cup sugar

¾ teaspoon salt

Add the onions and spice bag, and simmer for 5 minutes, stirring often. Discard the spice bag. Pack the hot onions into hot half-pint jars and add the hot solution. See *Putting Up Pickles*, 96. Leave ½-inch headspace, 12, and process for 10 minutes, 14.

Pickled Red or Golden Beets

About three 1-pint jars

Lovage's deeper-than-celery flavor is wonderful with beets (above). So are the flavors of tarragon and dill. Beets vary in their weight-to-volume ratio, so expect yields to vary.

Wash, then trim the tops and roots to 1 inch:

1½ to 2½ pounds red or golden beets of uniform size, from 1 to 2½ inches wide

Cover with boiling water and simmer just until tender. Drain, discarding the liquid. Remove the stems, roots, and skins. Leave baby beets under 1½ inches whole. Using a crinkle cutter, cut large beets into ¼-inch thick slices. Peel and thinly slice:

6 ounces 2- to 2½-inch onions, preferably white

Combine in a large, deep skillet and bring to a boil, stirring until the sugar is dissolved:

2 cups cider vinegar
¼ cup bottled lemon juice
¾ cup water
⅔ cup sugar
2 teaspoons black peppercorns
¾ teaspoon salt

Add the beets and onions and simmer for 5 minutes, stirring often. During the last minute, stir in:

⅓ cup finely chopped lovage or other fresh herb

Pack the vegetables into hot pint jars and add the hot vinegar solution. See *Putting Up Pickles*, 96. Leave ½-inch headspace, 12, and process for 30 minutes, 14.

End-of-the-Garden Sweet Pickle Mix

About six 1-pint jars

Husk and wash:

4 medium ears yellow corn

Boil for 5 minutes, then cut the kernels from the cob. Wash, trim the ends, and cut crosswise into ¼-inch-thick slices:

1 pound young zucchini or cucumbers

Wash, trim the ends, and cut into 2-inch pieces:

8 ounces tender snap beans

Wash, peel, and using a crinkle cutter, cut crosswise into ¼-inch-thick slices:

8 ounces tender carrots

Wash and cut into 1-inch florets:

8 ounces cauliflower

Wash, core, seed, and cut into

2 x ½-inch strips:

8 ounces bell peppers, both red and green

Wash and peel:

8 ounces pearl onions

Combine and stir until the salt is dissolved:

8 cups water

½ cup salt

Pour over all the vegetables in a large bowl. Place a plate on the vegetables to keep them submerged and refrigerate for 12 to 18 hours. Drain, but do not rinse. Combine in a large, deep skillet and boil gently for 3 minutes, stirring until the sugar is dissolved:

3 cups cider vinegar

3 cups white vinegar

¼ cup bottled lemon juice

2 cups sugar

2 tablespoons celery seeds

1 tablespoon red pepper flakes

½ teaspoon ground tumeric

Add the vegetables along with:

¼ cup chopped fresh basil

Bring to a simmer over high heat, stirring often, until the largest, thickest pieces are thoroughly hot. Use a slotted spoon to pack the vegetables into hot pint jars. Add the hot vinegar solution, stirring to mix the seeds and chopped herb. See *Putting Up Pickles*, 96. Leave ½-inch headspace, 12, and process for 15 minutes, 14.

Yellow Cucumber Pickles

About seven 1-pint jars

This recipe is adapted from the 1931 edition of JOY. Use large, yellow, mature cucumbers. Serve these pickles chilled with meat.

Wash, peel, halve lengthwise, and scrape out the seeds from:

15 pounds large yellow pickling cucumbers

Cut into 2½ x 1½ x ¾-inch strips. Make a brine of:

5½ quarts water

2 cups salt

Stir until the salt is dissolved and pour over the cucumber strips in a large bowl. Place a plate on the cucumbers to keep them submerged and let stand at room temperature for 12 hours. Drain, rinse, and drain again. Place in each hot pint jar (double the amount for quarts):

Two ⅓-inch cubes peeled horseradish

One ¼-inch piece red chili pepper

2 sprigs seeded dill flowers

1½ teaspoons mustard seeds

2 white peppercorns

Combine, bring to a boil, and stir until the sugar is dissolved:

6 cups cider vinegar

¾ cup water

¼ cup sugar

Divide between 2 or 3 large, shallow skillets, add the cucumber strips, and return just to a boil—do not cook longer, or the cucumbers will soften. Pack into the hot jars and add the hot vinegar solution. See *Putting Up Pickles*, 96. Leave ½-inch headspace, 12, and process pints for 10 minutes, quarts for 15 minutes, 14.

Sweet and Sour Spiced Gherkins

About six 1-pint jars

Wash, then slice ¹⁄₁₆ inch from the blossom ends, but leave ¼ inch of the stems on:

5 pounds 1½- to 2-inch West Indian gherkins or pickling cucumbers

Combine in a bowl:

12 cups water

1 cup salt

Stir until the salt is dissolved, then add the cucumbers. Place a plate on the cucumbers to keep them submerged and let stand at room temperature for 24 hours. Drain, cover the cucumbers with boiling water, and quickly drain again. Pack into hot pint jars. Heat in a saucepan, stirring until the sugar is dissolved:

4 cups cider vinegar

2¾ cups sugar

Tie in a cloth and add:

2 tablespoons mixed pickling spice, 93

Two 2-inch cinnamon sticks, broken

¼ teaspoon whole cloves

Bring just to a boil and remove the spice bag. Add the hot vinegar solution to the jars. See *Putting Up Pickles*, 96. Leave ½-inch headspace, 12, and process for 10 minutes, 14.

Quick Dill Pickles

About six 1-pint jars

Because the brine is weaker and the curing more rapid than traditional pickles, these are best enjoyed within a few months.

Wash:

4 pounds 4-inch pickling cucumbers

Halve lengthwise and pack into hot pint jars. (Cut longer cucumbers into 4-inch pieces, and fill the spaces in the jars with the scraps.) Combine in a saucepan and bring just to a boil, stirring until the salt is dissolved:

3 cups cider vinegar

2¼ cups water

¼ cup salt

Place in each jar:

1 clove garlic, peeled

1 teaspoon dill seeds

1 teaspoon mixed pickling spice, 93

6 black peppercorns

Add the hot vinegar solution. See *Putting Up Pickles*, 96. Leave ½-inch headspace, 12, and process for 10 minutes, 14.

Low-Salt Sweet Cucumber Slices

About four 1-pint jars

These pickles (above) are crunchy, delicious, and low in sodium.

Wash and trim ⅛ inch from the ends of:

2 pounds 3- to 4-inch pickling cucumbers

Using a crinkle cutter, cut crosswise into ¼-inch-thick slices. Combine in a saucepan:

1⅔ cups white vinegar

3 cups sugar

1 tablespoon whole allspice

1 tablespoon celery seeds

¼ teaspoon ground turmeric

Cook, stirring, over medium heat until the sugar is dissolved; turn off the heat and cover the syrup. Combine in a large, deep skillet:

4 cups white vinegar

½ cup sugar

1 tablespoon mustard seeds

1 tablespoon salt

Add the cucumbers and simmer just until their green turns from bright to dull, 5 to 7 minutes, stirring frequently—do not let the slices soften. Meanwhile, bring the syrup to a boil. Drain the slices, discarding the liquid. Pack the hot slices into hot pint jars and add the hot syrup. See *Putting Up Pickles*, 96. Leave ½-inch headspace, 12, and process for 10 minutes, 14.

Cornichons

About eight 1-pint jars

In France, these tiny cucumber pickles always accompany pâtés and cold meats, and are exceedingly sharp. This recipe makes a milder cornichon, which seems to suit more palates. If you enjoy the classic bite, use 6 cups vinegar in this recipe and omit the water. Standard pickling cucumbers can also be prepared this way. Cure 1 month before serving for true cornichon flavor.

Wash, then cut a thin slice from the blossom ends, but leave ¼-inch of the stems on:

5½ pounds cucumbers, 1¼ to 1½ inches long, preferably bred for cornichons

(For standard-size cucumbers, slice crosswise every 1½ inches, then quarter lengthwise.)

Make a brine of:

8 cups water

½ cup salt

Stir until the salt is dissolved and pour over the cucumbers in a large bowl. Place a plate on the cucumbers to keep them submerged and let stand at room temperature for 12 hours. Drain, rinse, and drain again. Dry in a clean towel. Tightly pack the cucumbers in the hot jars, adding to each pint (double the amounts for quarts):

A few sprigs fresh tarragon

½ teaspoon mustard seeds (optional)

5 white peppercorns

Combine in a saucepan and bring just to a boil, stirring until the salt is dissolved.

5¼ cups cider vinegar

4¼ cups water

⅓ cup salt

Pour the hot vinegar solution over the cucumbers in the jars. See *Putting Up Pickles*, 96. Leave ½-inch headspace, 12, and process pints for 10 minutes, quarts for 15 minutes, 14.

Bread-and-Butter Pickles

About five 1-pint jars

This recipe offers stovetop or microwave cooking options.

Wash, then slice ⅛ inch from the ends of:

2½ pounds pickling cucumbers

Cut crosswise into ¼-inch-thick slices. Peel, then cut the same way:

1 pound 2- to 2½-inch onions, preferably red

Combine the cucumbers and onions in a large bowl along with:

3 tablespoons salt

Mix well to dissolve the salt. Cover with a clean wet towel, then top with 2 inches of ice. Refrigerate for 3 to 4 hours. Discard the ice; drain the vegetables, rinse, and drain again. Combine in a 4-quart or larger microwave-safe bowl (or a saucepan if using the stovetop):

2 cups white vinegar

2 cups sugar

1 tablespoon mustard seeds

1 teaspoon red pepper flakes (optional)

¾ teaspoon celery seeds

¾ teaspoon ground turmeric

¼ teaspoon ground cloves

Stir until the sugar is dissolved. Cover with waxed paper and microwave on high (or cook uncovered on a burner) until the syrup boils. Add the vegetables, stir to mix, and microwave on medium-high until the syrup just begins to boil. Using a slotted spoon, pack the hot slices into hot pint jars and then add the hot syrup. See *Putting Up Pickles*, 96. Leave ½-inch headspace, 12, and process for 10 minutes, 14.

SUMMER SQUASH BREAD-AND-BUTTER PICKLES

Prepare Bread-and-Butter Pickles, left, substituting 1- to 2-inch wide zucchini or yellow crookneck squash for the cucumbers.

Cranberry-Pickled Pears

About two 1-pint jars

The flesh of whole Seckel and Forelle pears turns a beautiful color in this recipe (opposite). Core before adding to the syrup if using hard 2-inch pears such as Kieffer or Sand. When using hard large pears, quarter, core, and simmer in water for 10 to 15 minutes before adding to the syrup.

Wash and pick over:

1½ pounds cranberries

For the syrup, combine the berries in a large, deep skillet that will just accommodate the pears with:

2¼ cups cider vinegar

3 cups packed light brown sugar

⅛ teaspoon salt

Cook, stirring, over medium heat until the sugar is dissolved, then simmer for 10 minutes. Strain the syrup through a fine-mesh sieve back into the pan, pressing the juice from the berries. Tie in a cloth and add:

12 whole allspice

Two 2-inch cinnamon sticks

½ teaspoon whole cloves

Wash, peel, remove the blossom ends but leave the stems on, and place in an antibrowning solution, 22:

2 pounds small, firm, ripe pears of uniform size (see note)

Drain the pears. Return the syrup to a boil and add the pears. Simmer until just tender, 15 to 25 minutes, constantly pushing the pears under the syrup with a wooden spoon— do not overcook. Remove from the heat and pour into a shallow dish. Cover loosely with waxed paper, and plump in the refrigerator overnight, 59. Bring to a simmer, stirring; remove the spice bag. Pack the hot pears tightly (so they will not float) in hot pint jars, then add the hot syrup. See *Putting Up Pickles*, 96. Leave ½-inch headspace, 12, and process for 20 minutes, 14.

PICKLED CRAB APPLES

Crabapples are small and very tart. They are excellent for pickles and jellies because they contain so much pectin. Prepare *Cranberry-Pickled Pears, left,* substituting crab apples for the pears. Wash crab apples; remove blossom ends but do not peel or remove stems. Prick the fruit in several places with a thin skewer. Prepare the syrup, substituting an additional 1 cup apple cider for the cranberries. Bring the syrup to a boil in a large, deep skillet. Add the apples without crowding and simmer until just tender; remove with a slotted spoon. Repeat with more apples as necessary. Plump overnight in the refrigerator, 59. Bring to a simmer, stirring. Pack the hot apples into hot pint jars and add the hot syrup. Process for 30 minutes, 14.

Pickled Peaches

About twelve 1-pint jars

Another classic from the first edition of JOY. Tree-ripened peaches produce the fullest flavor.

Wash, peel, and place in an antibrowning solution, 22:

16 pounds small clingstone peaches

Press into each peach, evenly spaced:

3 whole cloves

Combine in a saucepan and bring to a boil, stirring until the sugar is dissolved:

8 cups cider vinegar

12 cups sugar

Simmer for 5 minutes. Skim and then add:

Six 2-inch cinnamon sticks tied in a cloth

Drain the peaches. Return the syrup to a boil and add the peaches. Simmer until just tender enough to be pierced with a thin skewer, about 5 minutes—do not overcook. Remove from the heat and pour into a shallow dish. Cover loosely with waxed paper, and plump in the refrigerator overnight, 59. Bring to a boil, stirring; remove the spice bag. Pack the hot peaches into hot pint jars, then add the hot syrup. See *Putting Up Pickles*, 96. Leave ½-inch headspace, 12, and process for 20 minutes, 14.

PICKLED APRICOTS

Sixteen 1-pint jars

Prepare *Pickled Peaches, left,* substituting unpeeled apricots of any size for the peaches.

Pickled Watermelon Rind

About eight to ten 1-pint jars

Food-grade oil of cinnamon and oil of cloves are available at some health food stores and pharmacies and keep their pungency a long time in a cool, dark, dry place. In this recipe (above), plumping is mandatory.

Wash, then cut lengthwise into eighths:

20 pounds slightly underripe citron melons or watermelons with thick, firm rinds

Discard the citron melon flesh or refrigerate the watermelon flesh for another use. Scrape out all but a thin line of flesh (it will not get crisp), then peel off the outer green skin. Cut the rind into 1-inch-wide diamonds or squares or stamp out with a 1-inch-wide cookie cutter. Parboil in water until the pieces are tender yet slightly crisp at the center when pierced with a skewer, about 10 minutes—do not overcook. Drain and place in a large bowl. Combine in a large, deep skillet and bring just to a boil, stirring until the sugar is dissolved:

7 cups sugar
2 cups white vinegar
½ teaspoon oil of cinnamon
¼ teaspoon oil of cloves

Pour the syrup over the rind, just covering it. Cover and plump in the refrigerator overnight, 59. In the morning, drain the syrup back into the pan, bring just to a boil, and pour again over the rind. Cover and plump overnight as before. On the third morning, bring the syrup and rind to a boil. Pack the hot rind into hot pint jars, then add the hot syrup. The flavor of this pickle may be varied by placing in each jar:

1 star anise (optional)
1 to 2 teaspoons chopped preserved ginger or candied lemon peel (optional)

See *Putting Up Pickles*, 96. Leave ½-inch headspace, 12, and process for 10 minutes, 14.

Pickled Lemon-Melon Rind

About nine ½-pint jars

Any firm-fleshed muskmelon, tropical melon, or true cantaloupe will make these delicious pickles. Plumping is mandatory in this recipe.

Slice into the thinnest possible rounds, saving the juice but discarding the seeds:

8 ounces lemons

Combine in a saucepan with:

3 cups water

Simmer until tender, 15 to 30 minutes. Strain the lemons, reserving the cooking liquid. Wash, then halve and slice lengthwise:

5½ pounds slightly underripe melons

Remove the rind and seed, then cut the flesh into 1-inch cubes. Combine in a large, deep skillet:

2 cups lemon cooking liquid

3 cups white vinegar

5 cups sugar

2 tablespoons mixed pickling spice, 93, tied in a cloth

Bring to a boil, stirring until the sugar is dissolved, then simmer for 5 minutes. Add the melon and lemons. Simmer, stirring occasionally, until the melon darkens to a pumpkin color and begins to become translucent, 30 to 45 minutes. Remove from the heat and pour into a shallow dish. Cover loosely with waxed paper, and plump in the refrigerator overnight, 59. Bring the syrup to a simmer, stirring; remove the spice bag. Pack the hot fruit into hot half-pint jars, then add the hot syrup. See *Putting Up Pickles*, 96. Leave ½-inch headspace, 12, and process for 10 minutes, 14.

NETTED MELONS

America's cantaloupe, muskmelon, Persian, and nutmeg melons all have netted rinds. Choose those in which the netting is pronounced and the fragrance is sweet. The melon's flesh should be musky and orange. In Europe, and botanically speaking, true cantaloupes have another shape. They have a smooth, hard rind and may be lightly fluted. Their orange, green, or pink flesh is intensely sweet and perfumed. The great French Charentais melon is the most prominent in this group. If a melon has no fruity perfume at the smooth (blossom) end, do not buy it. Choose melons that are heaviest for their size, with no soft spots, mold, or cracks and no strong aroma indicating over-ripeness. If, when you gently shake a melon, seeds rattle, chances are the melon is too ripe for pickling.

Pickled Sour Cherries

About 1 pint per 1 to 1¼ pounds cherries

This quick-pickling technique takes little effort. For best results, maintain an air temperature between 70° and 75°F. Montmorency, a morello, is the principal sour cherry in this country. It is predominantly grown in New England, around the Great Lakes, and on the Great Plains.

Stem, pit, and place in a heavy crock, 94:

Sour cherries

Cover with:

White vinegar

Weight to keep the cherries submerged and then cover. Let stand for 24 hours. Drain, discarding the vinegar, and measure the volume of cherries. Measure an equal volume amount of:

Sugar

Gently mix the cherries and the sugar in the crock until most of the sugar has dissolved. Cover with a thick, clean towel. The next day, stir gently until the sugar is dissolved to thoroughly blend the fruit and syrup. Weight and cover. Stir daily for 1 week after adding the sugar. Bring to a boil, stirring. Pack the cherries into hot pint jars and add the hot syrup. See *Putting Up Pickles*, 96. Leave ½-inch headspace, 12, and process for 15 minutes, 14.

Salting

For thousands of years, food has been preserved with salt. Salting is also known as long brining, fermentation, or curing. Strictly speaking, vinegar is not needed because the food produces its own acid during fermentation. However, you will notice that sometimes there is a little vinegar in a brine recipe to give a kick start and margin of safety to the fermentation.

All food in brine must be weighted so it will stay submerged and pickle properly. One very simple method for long brining is to make a weight by placing one large sealable plastic freezer bag inside another. Fill the inside bag with pickling brine and close the ends of both bags securely—use brine instead of water, in case the bags leak or break. Place on top of the food in the crock. Use enough weight to sink the food 1 to 2 inches beneath the brine. The bag (or bags) must completely cover and submerge the food to prevent the formation of scum.

If filled plastic bags are not used, cover the food with clean, wet muslin or cheesecloth, tucking the cloth against the sides of the container. Place a clean, dry plate on top of the cloth—it should just fit inside the container. Set clean, tightly capped water-filled jars on top of the plate. Check for scum every day, and remove it from the surface and around the sides of the crock as it forms.

As precautions, use only plastic, wooden, or stainless-steel implements when stirring or retrieving pickling foods, and use tongs instead of your hands. Even the cleanest of hands can spread bacteria. A spotless heavy bath towel to cover the crock at room temperature will keep out dust, insects, and other contaminants. A heavy, tight-fitting lid is best for a container in the refrigerator.

Crock-Cured Dill Pickles

About three 1-quart jars

Although fully cured pickles take weeks, after about 1 week, pickles are called "new dill," and, to many, are at their prime. This recipe fills a 1-gallon crock. The leaves add crunch but are not essential.

Wash, then slice ¹⁄₁₆ inch from the blossom ends, but leave ¼ inch of the stems on:

4 pounds 4-inch pickling cucumbers

Wash and pat dry:

8 cups unsprayed grape or cherry leaves (optional)

4 to 6 sprigs fresh dill

Wash, peel, and thinly slice:

2 to 6 large garlic cloves, peeled

Measure:

1 tablespoon to ⅓ cup mixed pickling spice, according to taste, 93

Loosely layer leaves and seasonings with the cucumbers in a 1-gallon crock, leaving space for air between the cucumbers. Start and end with the leaves and the seasonings. Combine, stirring until the salt is dissolved:

8 cups water

½ cup salt

¼ cup cider vinegar

Pour over the cucumbers. Weight to keep the cucumbers submerged and cover, above. Check for scum daily, and stir every 2 to 3 days. Test after 1 week to see if the pickles are to your taste. New dills—ready when their color has changed from bright green to dull yellowish green—should be tightly packed in hot sterilized jars, covered with brine, and refrigerated. Fully fermented pickles may be refrigerated in the crock and will keep for 4 to 6 months. Promptly remove any surface scum and mold on refrigerated pickles, or they will quickly spoil. The best way to keep pickles is to can them, although it will alter their crispness and flavor. Pour the brine into a saucepan, bring slowly to a boil, and simmer for 5 minutes. Pack the pickles into hot jars and add the hot brine. See *Putting Up Pickles*, 96. Leave ½-inch headspace, 12, and process pints for 10 minutes, quarts for 15 minutes, 14.

CROCK-CURED GREEN TOMATO DILL PICKLES

Prepare Crock-Cured Dill Pickles, left, substituting 5 pounds small, firm green tomatoes for the cucumbers. Process as directed above.

Sauerkraut

About 1 scant quart per 5 pounds cabbage

Fabulous to eat and an adventure to make, home-cured sauerkraut has little in common with its factory counterpart. Prepare 5 pounds of cabbage at a time. Remove the outer leaves, wash under cold running water, and drain:

5 pounds mature, firm, fresh cabbage, any but Savoy

Quarter and remove the cores. Thinly slice the cabbage and place in a bowl along with:

3 tablespoons salt

Mix well, then let stand a few minutes to wilt (this makes packing easier). Pack firmly and evenly in a stone crock or other container as directed for *Salting, opposite.* Press down until the juice rises to the surface. If, after pressing, the juice does not rise above the shreds, make a brine of:

1½ tablespoons salt per 4 cups water

Bring to a boil, cool, then add to the crock. Weight to keep the cabbage submerged, and cover, opposite. The next day, the presence of gas bubbles will indicate that fermentation has begun. Check the cabbage once or twice a week. If scum develops, remove it immediately, or the kraut will spoil. When the bubbles stop in 3 to 6 weeks, fermentation is complete. Fully fermented sauerkraut keeps in a covered jar in the refrigerator for several months as long as the cabbage is always completely covered by liquid. For longer keeping, bring the kraut and liquid slowly to a simmer, stirring often—do not boil. Firmly pack the kraut in hot jars, then add the hot brine solution. See *Putting Up Pickles,* 96. Leave ½-inch headspace, 12, and process pints for 10 minutes, quarts for 15 minutes, 14.

CABBAGE

Although cabbages are in the market year-round, if you watch closely you will see that they change with the seasons. Early or summer cabbages, harvested June through October, are cone shaped; they weigh 2 to 2½ pounds and have tender, juicy, mild leaves. Cabbages that mature from mid-October through March have flat or round heads and weigh 3 to 15 pounds; their flavor is well developed. Those picked after a hard autumn frost are sweetest. Fineness of flavor in cabbages is indicated by thickness of leaves— the thinner, the better. Savoy cabbages—those with ruffled crinkly leaves—have the thinnest leaves and incomparable flavor; unfortunately, their slim leaves make them unsuitable for sauerkraut, which requires hardy leaves. As pretty as they are, red cabbages have thicker leaves than green cabbages, and their flavor is less interesting. Select cabbages that are heavy for their size and have bright, crisp leaves with no signs of yellowing, cuts, or bruises. Store cabbage in perforated plastic vegetable bags in the refrigerator crisper.

Salt-Cured Black Olives

About 1 pint per 1 pound of cured olives

You may choose to rinse some of the salt off the olives before serving. Line a slatted wooden box with clean burlap and set it on a tarp—dark tannin from the olives will stain. Rinse, then pat dry, handling carefully:

Fully ripe, small, dark uncured olives

Place a layer of olives 1 olive deep in the box. Sprinkle with a layer of:

Rock salt

The salt should just cover the olives. Continue layering the olives and salt, finishing with the salt. Cover the box with burlap and let stand for 24 hours in a bright, airy place out of full sun. Wearing rubber gloves, use your hands to gently but thoroughly mix the olives and salt every day or two—the olives can spoil if this is not done faithfully. They will be ready in about 4 to 6 weeks. Remove the olives from the salt, brushing it off. (Do not wash off the salt, as what remains helps preserve the olives.) Pack them into sterilized jars, adding to each:

1 fresh bay leaf (optional)
Ground white pepper to taste (optional)
Olive oil to cover

Cover tightly and store in a cool, dark, dry place.

ABOUT
DRYING

*F*ew climates are well suited to the sun drying of fruits and vegetables, as ancient as this custom is. We include here three simple recipes for drying in any home: Room-Dried Herbs and Chili Peppers, Fruit Leather, and Jerky. *Should you wish to explore further drying foods, we recommend you buy an electric dehydrator and follow the manufacturer's instructions.*

Room-Dried Herbs and Chili Peppers

Food can be dried in any warm room with good circulation of air on the dry side. Optimum conditions are temperatures above 85°F and humidity below 60 percent. A broad south-facing window sill will be most likely to provide these conditions. Herbs and chili peppers are well suited to this method.

HERBS

Remove any dead and bruised blossoms and leaves. If the herbs are dusty, place them in a colander and dip in cool water, then shake off the excess water gently. Pat dry on a towel. It is important to dry herbs thoroughly, as they mildew easily. Tie stalks into small bunches with cotton string and place each bunch upside down inside a large paper bag that has ventilation holes punched all over. Tie the neck of the bag tightly, and hang the bag with leaves facing downward in a warm, airy place. The bag keeps light from degrading the leaves and flowers, and catches any seeds that pop.

CHILI PEPPERS

For chili peppers from the garden, pull up the plant, shake off the earth from the roots, wipe the peppers with a damp cloth, and hang the plant upside down in a ventilated paper bag or by itself. This technique also works with annual herb plants such as the basils, German chamomile, and sweet marjoram. When the herb leaves and flowers are brittle, pull them off the stems over a sheet of waxed paper. The pieces are best left whole.

For chili peppers from the market, thread a stout needle with an arm's length of string and make a big knot at one end. String the peppers on the line, pushing the needle through the stems. Leave ½ inch or so between each pepper. Tie a loop on the top and hang the peppers in a dark but airy part of the room. A chili pepper is finished drying when it is brittle.

Jerky

About 14 servings

Ounce for ounce, jerky has 166 percent more protein, 150 percent more calories, and 50 percent less fat than the leanest grilled meat. If you are a meat eater, jerky need be the only protein on a camping trip. Hydrate strips in cold water overnight, then chop and simmer in a soup or stew. Or eat it as is.

Trim all fat, membrane, and gristle from:

1 pound beef eye round, bottom round, or flank steak, or comparably lean cut of game

Wrap in plastic wrap and freeze until partially frozen, 2 to 4 hours. Use a sharp knife to cut with the grain: for crisp sticks, cut into ⅛-inch-thick slices; for chewy jerky, cut ¼-inch-thick slices. Arrange the meat strips close together on waxed paper. Mix together:

4 teaspoons fine-grained sea salt
4 teaspoons sugar
1 to 2 teaspoons ground black pepper (optional)

Lightly sprinkle about half this mixture over the strips. Turn the strips over and repeat. Preheat the oven to 140°F or the lowest setting. Stack the strips and cut lengthwise 1 to 1½ inches wide and 4 to 6 inches long, or as desired. Rub a clean oven rack with oil and place the strips on it without touching one another. Set the rack in the center of the oven. Prop open the oven door 2 to 6 inches. Bake until the strips are very dry but still slightly flexible, bending before they break. Remove the rack from the oven. After cooling for a few minutes, remove the strips from the rack. Cool, and then pack in airtight containers. Store in a cool, dry place.

Fruit Leather

1 cup puree will make 2 to 3 servings

Fruit leather is a sheet of pureed fruit that has been dried. Fresh fruits that make excellent leathers are apples, apricots, berries, sweet cherries, nectarines, peaches, pears, pineapples, and plums. An electric dehydrator is the easiest way to dry a fruit leather. Drying can also be done in the oven.

Cover a drying tray or baking sheet with plastic freezer wrap, extending it over the edges.

Peel and seed or pit:

Ripe fruit

Chop fruits that darken when exposed to the air—apples, apricots, nectarines, peaches, and pears. Place the fruit in a saucepan, and cook, stirring, over low heat, until a candy thermometer reaches 190°F. Let cool thoroughly, then puree in a blender, food processor, or food mill, straining, if necessary, to make a fine, smooth, fairly liquidy puree. If the puree is very thick, thin it with:

Fruit juice

If the fruit needs sweetening or additional flavor, add:

A little corn syrup, honey, sugar, or lemon or orange juice

(Corn syrup prevents the formation of crystals, so it is best for long storage. Saccharin-based sweeteners can also be used.) Spread the puree on the tray ⅛ inch thick in the center and ¼ inch thick around the edges. Dry in a dehydrator at 135°F, or in the oven at 140°F or the lowest setting. The fruit is ready when the sheet is leathery and not sticky. While still warm, roll up the leather jelly-roll fashion in the plastic wrap. If desired, use scissors to cut the roll into serving pieces. Cool, and then pack in airtight containers. For longest keeping, refrigerate or freeze.

NECTARINES

Nectarines, even at their best, are sometimes not as juicy as peaches, but their flavors can be sublime. If you use nectarines in a recipe that calls for a bit of juice, add some orange or pineapple juice. Nectarines are tricky to pit neatly, but protecting the condition of the flesh is not an issue when making fruit leather.

ABOUT
CONDIMENTS

*C*ondiments are quick and easy to prepare, and their intense flavors can make even a plain broiled chicken breast into an interesting meal. Serve these condiments as a garnish for soups or stews, on steamed vegetables, with grains and beans, with pasta, grilled foods, tortilla chips, breads, or crackers.

From left: Apple Chutney, 120, and Pear Chutney, 120

Putting Up Condiments

We make these large-quantity, old-fashioned recipes for gifts. Do not halve recipe amounts; simmering in smaller batches affects flavor, texture, and most importantly, the critical acid content. There are two methods of keeping your homemade condiments—refrigeration and canning.

REFRIGERATION

Condiments can be cooled, covered, and stored in the refrigerator for 2 to 4 weeks.

CANNING

Please read the directions for proper and safe canning, 8 to 19, before proceeding. The condiments in this section may be safely put up in a boiling-water canner, 14.

For the canner, any large pot will do, as long as it is at least 2½ inches taller than the jars being processed and has a lid. Place a rack on the bottom to let water circulate. Set the pot over just one burner, fill half full with hot water, and bring to a simmer (180°F). Use only defect-free Mason-type glass jars and the two-piece vacuum caps manufactured specifically for these jars. The lids must be new, but the rings can be reused until they rust or warp. See *Equipment*, 11. Condiments are best packed in pint or half-pint jars (the processing time is the same for both). Heat the jars by filling them with very hot water; pour simmering water over the lids in a bowl. Fill and cap one jar at a time. Pack lightly with hot food, leaving the required headspace; see *Packing Jars*, 12. Force out any air bubbles by sliding a clean plastic spatula between the food and the sides of the jar, 13. Wipe the rim and threads of the jar with a clean damp cloth. Set on the lid and screw the ring on firmly—stop turning when you feel resistance. Immediately lower the jar into the kettle. Jars should not touch.

Process the jars, adding or removing boiling water so the level remains 1 inch above the jar tops. Cover the kettle and bring to a rolling boil over highest heat. When the water boils, set the timer (If canning above sea level, see *High-Altitude Canning*, 15). Adjust the heat to maintain a gentle boil, and maintain the water level. When the jars have boiled for the recommended time, turn off the heat and lift the jars onto a towel in a draft-free place, placing them at least 1 inch apart. See *Cooling the Jars*, 16. Do not tighten the rings. Let the jars cool for 12 to 24 hours, then check the seal: Every lid should curve down slightly in the center and should stay depressed when pressed with a finger. If the seal has failed, refrigerate the jar at once and serve the contents within a few days. Label the sealed jars and store in a cool, dark, dry place. See *Storing Canned Goods*, 17. Familiarize yourself with the guidelines in *Checking for Spoilage*, 19.

Piccalilli

About five 1-pint jars

Remove a thin slice from each end, then chop:

5 pounds tender small cucumbers

Combine them in a large bowl with:

1⅓ pounds green bell peppers, cored, seeded, and chopped

1⅓ pounds onions, peeled and chopped

Stir together in another bowl until the salt is dissolved:

2½ quarts cool water

1 cup salt

Add the brine to the vegetables. Place a plate on the vegetables to keep them submerged, and refrigerate for 12 hours. Drain well. Combine and bring just to the boiling point, stirring until the sugar is dissolved:

1 quart cider vinegar

4 cups sugar

Tie in a moist square of cloth and add to the saucepan:

3 tablespoons whole mixed spices, such as pickling spices, 93

1½ teaspoons celery seeds

1½ teaspoons mustard seeds

Add the drained vegetables. Return to the boiling point. Stir in, if desired:

1 tablespoon plus 2 teaspoons red pepper flakes

Discard the spice bag. Pack the hot vegetables into hot jars and add the hot liquid. See *Putting Up Condiments*, *above*. Leave ½-inch headspace, 12, and process for 15 minutes, 14.

Green Tomato Relish

About six 1-pint jars

This recipe (above) is perfect for unripened tomatoes.

Combine in a large bowl:

8 pounds green tomatoes, thinly sliced

2¾ pounds onions, peeled and thinly sliced

Sprinkle with:

½ cup salt

Stir together well, cover, and refrigerate for 12 hours. Rinse in cold water and drain. Combine and bring to a boil, stirring until the sugar is dissolved:

1½ quarts cider vinegar

2 pounds brown sugar

Stir in:

2 pounds green bell peppers, cored, seeded, and sliced

1 pound red bell peppers, cored, seeded, and diced

6 cloves garlic, peeled and minced

1 tablespoon dry mustard

1½ teaspoons salt

Add the tomatoes and onions and stir together well. Tie in a moist square of cloth and add to the saucepan.

1 tablespoon whole cloves

1 tablespoon ground ginger

1½ teaspoons celery seeds

One 3-inch cinnamon stick, broken

Simmer, stirring often, until the tomatoes are translucent, about 1 hour. Discard the spice bag. Pack the hot vegetables into hot jars and add the hot liquid. See *Putting Up Condiments, opposite.* Leave ½-inch headspace, 12, and process for 15 minutes, 14.

Tart Corn Relish

About ten 1-pint jars

Crunchy corn and bright colors and flavors make this relish (opposite) especially prized. Use only fresh corn. Remove the husks and silks, and blanch for 5 minutes in boiling salted water (1 teaspoon salt to every 1 quart water):

18 medium ears yellow or bicolor corn

Dip in cold water, then pat dry. Cut the kernels from the cobs, without scraping, into a very large container. Chop and then add to the corn:

8 ounces green bell peppers, cored and seeded

1 pound red bell peppers, cored and seeded

4 ounces mild green chili peppers, cored and seeded

1½ pounds red onions, peeled

12 ounces green or red cabbage

Stir in:

5 cups cider vinegar

1 cup sugar

1 cup water

½ cup bottled lemon juice

3 tablespoons chopped fresh dill, or 1½ teaspoons dried dill

2 tablespoons salt

2 teaspoons yellow mustard seeds

2 teaspoons ground turmeric

1 teaspoon celery seeds

Mix until well blended. Whisk until smooth in a small bowl, and then divide in half:

1 cup water

½ cup all-purpose flour

Cook the vegetables in 2 batches. Bring the vegetables to a boil over high heat, then reduce the heat and simmer, stirring often, for 10 minutes. Stir the reserved flour mixture into each pan, and cook, stirring. Once the mixture thickens, cook for 10 minutes more, stirring often. Pack the hot mixture into hot jars. See *Putting Up Condiments*, 116. Leave ½-inch headspace, 12, and process for 15 minutes, 14.

Chow-Chow

About ten 1-pint jars

Another JOY original, this recipe appeared in the first edition. Chow-chow can be served as a creamy relish or a crunchy cool sauce. Remove a thin slice from each end, then slice crosswise ¼ inch thick:

2 pounds unpeeled 4-inch pickling cucumbers

Stir together in a large bowl until the salt is dissolved:

5 cups cold water

½ cup salt

Pour over the cucumbers. Place a plate on the cucumbers to keep them submerged, and refrigerate for 12 hours. For the sauce, combine and stir until the sugar is dissolved:

2½ quarts cider vinegar

2½ cups sugar

Stir together in a medium bowl until smooth:

1½ cups all-purpose flour

6 tablespoons dry mustard

1½ tablespoons ground turmeric

3 tablespoons celery seeds

Slowly whisk about 2 cups of the vinegar mixture into the flour mixture until smooth. Bring the remaining vinegar mixture to a simmer over low heat. Slowly whisk in the flour mixture. Cook, whisking constantly, until smooth and simmering. Remove from the heat, cover, and reserve. Cut into ½-inch pieces or dice, to make 3 quarts:

1½ pounds firm green tomatoes, cored

1½ pounds green bell peppers, cored and seeded

1 pound tender young snap peas, trimmed

Combine them in a large saucepan with:

1½ pounds tender cauliflower, cut into bite-sized florets

Blanch for 1 minute in boiling water, peel, and then add to the vegetables:

8 ounces pearl onions

Pour boiling salted water (1 teaspoon salt to every 1 quart water) over the vegetables to cover. Return to a boil, then drain thoroughly. Also drain thoroughly the reserved cucumbers. Add them to the vegetables and stir together well. Heat the mustard sauce to boiling and stir into the hot vegetables. Season to taste with:

Salt

Pack the hot mixture into hot jars. See *Putting Up Condiments*, 116. Leave ½-inch headspace, 12, and process for 15 minutes, 14.

Apple Chutney

About six 1-pint jars

Wonderfully tangy.
Stir together:

10 medium-large green apples, peeled, cored, and chopped

4 red bell peppers, cored, seeded, and chopped

3 cups seeded Muscat or large, dark seedless raisins

2 thin-skinned lemons, seeded and finely chopped

½ cup chopped peeled fresh ginger

2 cloves garlic, peeled and minced

4½ cups packed light brown sugar

4 cups cider vinegar

2 teaspoons salt, or to taste

½ teaspoon ground red pepper

Bring to a simmer, partially cover, and cook over low heat until thick, about 2 hours. Stir often—especially toward the end—to prevent scorching. Pack the hot chutney into hot jars. See *Putting Up Condiments*, 116. Leave ¼-inch headspace, 12, and process for 10 minutes, 14.

Pear Chutney

About five 1-pint jars

Ideal with pork, turkey, and game birds.
Zest and juice:

6 large oranges

Combine the zest and juice in a saucepan with:

2½ cups cider vinegar

2 pounds dark brown sugar

2 tablespoons ground coriander

2 tablespoons yellow mustard seeds

Four 3-inch cinnamon sticks, broken into 1-inch pieces

One 3-inch dried red chili pepper, crumbled

½ teaspoon ground cloves

½ teaspoon salt

4 pounds underripe pears, peeled, cored, and cut into ½-inch-thick slices

Stir the slices to coat them with the syrup. Add:

1 pound ripe tomatoes, peeled, seeded, and chopped, or drained canned plum tomatoes, chopped

12 ounces dark raisins

12 ounces golden raisins

1 large onion, peeled and minced

2 ounces fresh ginger, peeled and finely chopped

4 large cloves garlic, peeled and minced

Stir together well. Bring to a simmer,

partially cover, and stir often, pushing the pears beneath the syrup. After about 1½ hours, stir in:

1 cup thawed frozen unsweetened apple juice concentrate

1 cup water

Simmer, uncovered, stirring often, until the mixture is thick, dark, and syrupy and the pears are translucent, 1½ hours more. If desired, stir in:

1 tablespoon ground coriander (optional)

Pack the hot chutney into hot jars. See *Putting Up Condiments*, 116. Leave ¼-inch headspace, 12, and process for 10 minutes, 14.

Tomato Chutney

About eighteen 1-pint jars

Combine:

8 quarts chopped peeled ripe tomatoes

1 quart chopped peeled onions

1 quart chopped peeled green apples

1 pound seeded Muscat raisins or large dark seedless raisins

1 pound golden raisins

1½ pounds dark brown sugar

1½ pounds light brown sugar

1½ quarts cider vinegar

¼ cup yellow mustard seeds

2 tablespoons ground cloves

1 tablespoon ground allspice

1½ teaspoons ground red pepper

3 tablespoons salt, or to taste

Stir together well. Bring to a simmer,

partially cover, and cook over low heat until very thick and dark, 3 to 5 hours. Stir often—especially toward the end—to prevent scorching. Pack the hot chutney into hot jars. See *Putting Up Condiments*, 116. Leave ¼-inch headspace, 12, and process for 10 minutes, 14.

Green Mango Chutney

About thirteen ½-pint jars

Mango is the tropical fruit that is most associated with the word chutney. Green Mango Chutney (above) is good with chicken, veal, pork, fish, and all curried dishes.

Peel and cut into ½-inch-thick slices, separating the flesh from the seeds:

6½ pounds green mangoes

Peel and cut the slices in half crosswise, and combine with:

4 cups cider vinegar

Simmer, covered, until the mangoes are barely tender, about 20 minutes. Remove from the heat and stir in:

4 cups packed light brown sugar
8 ounces dried currants

Grind to a coarse powder in a spice grinder, coffee grinder, or blender, or with a mortar and pestle:

2½ tablespoons toasted yellow mustard seeds

Transfer to a blender or food processor. Cut into small pieces and add:

2 ounces fresh jalapeño or serrano chili peppers, cored and seeded
2 ounces garlic cloves, peeled
2 ounces fresh ginger, peeled

Pulse until finely chopped. Stir in, then pulse to a coarse paste:

3 tablespoons ground turmeric
2 tablespoons ground ginger
1½ tablespoons ground nutmeg
1 tablespoon ground allspice
2 teaspoons ground mace

2 teaspoons ground red pepper
2 teaspoons salt

Thoroughly stir this mixture into the mangoes. Bring to a simmer, stirring often, over low heat. Reduce the heat to the lowest setting and set the saucepan on a flame tamer. Cook, partially covered, until the mixture is the color of dark brown sugar and as thick as jam, about 3 hours. Stir every 10 minutes—more often toward the end—to prevent scorching. Pack the hot chutney into hot jars. See *Putting Up Condiments*, 116. Leave ¼-inch headspace, 12, and process for 10 minutes, 14.

Tomato Ketchup

About ten 1-pint jars

One taste of homemade Tomato Ketchup (above) and you will understand why it is worth taking the time to prepare it.

Combine in a large pot:

14 pounds ripe tomatoes, peeled and chopped

8 medium onions, peeled and sliced

2 red bell peppers, cored, seeded, and diced

Simmer over medium heat, stirring occasionally, until very soft. Puree through the medium blade of a food mill or push through a coarse-mesh strainer, then return to the pot. Stir in:

¾ cup packed light brown sugar

½ teaspoon dry mustard

Tie in a cloth and add to the tomato mixture:

One 3-inch cinnamon stick

1 tablespoon whole allspice

1 tablespoon whole cloves

1 tablespoon ground mace

1 tablespoon celery seeds

1 tablespoon black peppercorns

2 bay leaves

1 clove garlic, peeled

Bring the mixture to a rolling boil, then reduce to a simmer. Cook until the sauce is reduced by half, stirring often to prevent scorching. Remove and discard the spice bag. Stir in:

2 cups cider vinegar

Canning or pickling salt to taste, 92

Ground red pepper to taste (optional)

Reduce the heat and simmer, stirring almost constantly, for 10 minutes. Pack the hot ketchup into hot jars. See *Putting Up Condiments*, 116. Leave ⅛-inch headspace, 12, and process for 15 minutes, 14.

Blender Tomato Ketchup

About nine 1-pint jars

Process small batches in a blender until pureed, about 5 seconds each batch:

24 pounds ripe tomatoes, peeled and quartered
2 pounds onions, peeled and quartered
1 pound red bell peppers, cored, seeded, and cut into strips
1 pound green bell peppers, cored, seeded, and cut into strips

Stir together well and bring to a boil in a large pot, stirring often, over medium heat. Boil gently, stirring often and thoroughly, for 1 hour. Stir in:

9 cups cider vinegar
9 cups sugar
¼ cup canning or pickling salt, 92

Tie in a cloth and add to the tomato mixture:

3 tablespoons dry mustard
1½ tablespoons whole allspice
1½ tablespoons paprika
1½ tablespoons whole cloves
Two 3-inch cinnamon sticks

Boil gently and stir until the mixture is reduced by half and mounds up on a spoon with no separation of liquid and solids. Remove and discard the spice bag. Pack the hot ketchup into hot jars. See *Putting Up Condiments,* 116. Leave ⅛-inch headspace, 12, and process for 15 minutes, 14.

Mushroom Ketchup

Three ½-pint jars

This English condiment is thin, pungent, and deeply flavored.

Wipe clean and chop coarsely:

4 pounds mushrooms, preferably cremini

Spread out on a large, rimmed baking sheet lined with a layer of waxed paper and sprinkle with:

7 tablespoons coarse salt

Cover and refrigerate, stirring occasionally, for 2 to 3 days. Drain the mushrooms and rinse well, discarding the liquid. Combine in a large saucepan with:

1 cup red wine vinegar
⅔ cup cider vinegar
1 medium red onion, peeled and finely chopped
1 clove garlic, peeled and finely chopped
½ teaspoon ground black pepper
¼ teaspoon ground ginger
¼ teaspoon ground allspice
¼ teaspoon ground nutmeg

Bring to a boil, reduce the heat, and simmer, uncovered, stirring often, until very fragrant and flavorful, about 30 minutes. Strain into a clean saucepan, pressing out all the liquid. Bring to a simmer, then strain through a dampened cloth. Pack the hot ketchup into hot jars. See *Putting Up Condiments,* 116. Leave ⅛-inch headspace, 12, and process for 15 minutes, 14.

Chili Sauce

About eight 1-pint jars

Grind together in batches through the medium blade of a food mill or chop medium-fine in a food processor:

6 red bell peppers, cored, seeded, and coarsely chopped
6 large onions, peeled and coarsely chopped

Put in a large pot and stir in:

14 pounds ripe tomatoes, peeled, seeded, and chopped
3 cups cider vinegar
2 cups packed light brown sugar
2 tablespoons salt
1 tablespoon ground black pepper
1 tablespoon ground allspice
1 teaspoon ground cloves
1 teaspoon ground ginger
1 teaspoon ground cinnamon
1 teaspoon ground nutmeg
1 teaspoon celery seeds

Stir to blend thoroughly, then bring to a boil over medium heat. Simmer, stirring often to prevent scorching, until thick, about 3 hours. Adjust the seasonings to taste. Pack the hot sauce into hot jars. See *Putting Up Condiments,* 116. Leave ½-inch headspace, 12, and process for 15 minutes, 14.

Index

Bold type indicates that a recipe has an accompanying photograph.

Notes

Acknowledgments

Special thanks to my wife and editor in residence, Susan; our friend and editorial assistant, Cynthia Hoskin; our friend and great teacher, Missy Lynn; our capable and confident assistant, Maggie Green; and our friends and agents, Gene Winick and Sam Pinkus. Much appreciation also goes to Simon & Schuster, Scribner, and Weldon Owen for their devotion to this project. Thank you Carolyn, Susan, Beth, Rica, John, Terry, Roger, Gaye, Val, Norman, and all the other capable and talented folks who gave a part of themselves to the Joy of Cooking All About series.

My eternal appreciation goes to the food experts, writers, and editors whose contributions and collaborations are at the heart of JOY—especially Stephen Schmidt. He was to the 1997 edition what Chef Pierre Adrian was to Mother's final editions of JOY. Thank you one and all.

Ethan Becker

FOOD EXPERTS, WRITERS, AND EDITORS

Selma Abrams, Jody Adams, Samia Ahad, Bruce Aidells, Katherine Alford, Deirdre Allen, Pam Anderson, Elizabeth Andoh, Phillip Andres, Alice Arndt, John Ash, Nancy Baggett, Rick and Deann Bayless, Lee E. Benning, Rose Levy Beranbaum, Brigit Legere Binns, Jack Bishop, Carole Bloom, Arthur Boehm, Ed Brown, JeanMarie Brownson, Larry Catanzaro, Val Cipollone, Polly Clingerman, Elaine Corn, Bruce Cost, Amy Cotler, Brian Crawley, Gail Damerow, Linda Dann, Deirdre Davis, Jane Spencer Davis, Erica De Mane, Susan Derecskey, Abigail Johnson Dodge, Jim Dodge, Aurora Esther, Michele Fagerroos, Eva Forson, Margaret Fox, Betty Fussell, Mary Gilbert, Darra Goldstein, Elaine Gonzalez, Dorie Greenspan, Maria Guarnaschelli, Helen Gustafson, Pat Haley, Gordon Hamersley, Melissa Hamilton, Jessica Harris, Hallie Harron, Nao Hauser, William Hay, Larry Hayden, Kate Hays, Marcella Hazan, Tim Healea, Janie Hibler, Lee Hofstetter, Paula Hogan, Rosemary Howe, Mike Hughes, Jennifer Humphries, Dana Jacobi, Stephen Johnson, Lynne Rossetto Kasper, Denis Kelly, Fran Kennedy, Johanne Killeen and George Germon, Shirley King, Maya Klein, Diane M. Kochilas, Phyllis Kohn, Aglaia Kremezi, Mildred Kroll, Loni Kuhn, Corby Kummer, Virginia Lawrence, Jill Leigh, Karen Levin, Lori Longbotham, Susan Hermann Loomis, Emily Luchetti, Stephanie Lyness, Karen MacNeil, Deborah Madison, Linda Marino, Kathleen McAndrews, Alice Medrich, Anne Mendelson, Lisa Montenegro, Cindy Mushet, Marion Nestle, Toby Oksman, Joyce O'Neill, Suzen O'Rourke, Russ Parsons, Holly Pearson, James Peterson, Marina Petrakos, Mary Placek, Maricel Presilla, Marion K. Pruitt, Adam Rapoport, Mardee Haidin Regan, Peter Reinhart, Sarah Anne Reynolds, Madge Rosenberg, Nicole Routhier, Jon Rowley, Nancy Ross Ryan, Chris Schlesinger, Stephen Schmidt, Lisa Schumacher, Marie Simmons, Nina Simonds, A. Cort Sinnes, Sue Spitler, Marah Stets, Molly Stevens, Christopher Stoye, Susan Stuck, Sylvia Thompson, Jean and Pierre Troisgros, Jill Van Cleave, Patricia Wells, Laurie Wenk, Caroline Wheaton, Jasper White, Jonathan White, Marilyn Wilkenson, Carla Williams, Virginia Willis, John Willoughby, Deborah Winson, Lisa Yockelson.

Weldon Owen wishes to thank the following people for their generous assistance and support in producing this book: Desne Ahlers, Georgeanne Brennan and Jim Schrupp, Brynn Breuner, Ken DellaPenta, Kyrie Forbes, Arin Hailey, Norman Kolpas, Lou Pappas, and Ramsey Rickart. The photographers wish to thank Chrome Works, San Francisco.